On Santa Cruz Island

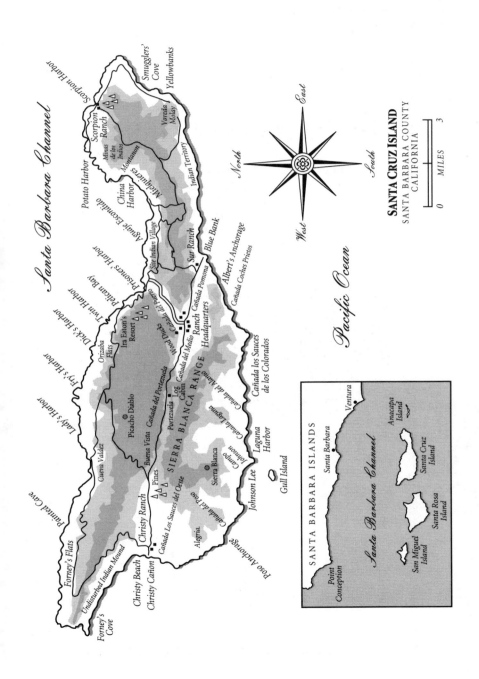

Santa Barbara Channel

Scorpion Harbor

Smugglers' Cove

Yellowbanks

Potato Harbor

Scorpion Ranch

Minas de los Indies

Montañon

Vareda Molay

Indian Territory

Mrilinires

China Harbor

Aguaje Escondido

Prisoners' Harbor

Site Indian Village

Sur Ranch

Blue Bank

Albert's Anchorage

Cañada Coches Prietos

Pelican Bay

Twin Harbor

Dick's Harbor

Fry's Harbor

Ira Eaton's Resort

Orizaba Flats

Cañada Pomona

Ranch Headquarters

Cañada del Medio

Cañada del Puerto

Woods

Log Cabin

Portezuela

Cañada del Puerto

Cañada los Sauces de los Colorados

Lady's Harbor

Picacho Diablo

Cañada de la Portezuela

Buena Vista

SIERRA BLANCA RANGE

Cañada del Alamo

Cañada Laguna

Laguna Harbor

Cueva Valdez

Pines

Camp Johnson

Sierra Blanca

Johnson Lee

Gull Island

Painted Cave

Christy Ranch

Cañada Los Sauces del Oeste

Cañada del Poso

Alegria

Poso Anchorage

Forney's Flats

Christy Beach

Christy Cañon

Undisturbed Indian Mound

Forney's Cove

Pacific Ocean

East

North

West

South

SANTA CRUZ ISLAND

SANTA BARBARA COUNTY
CALIFORNIA

0   MILES   3

SANTA BARBARA ISLANDS

Point Conception

Santa Barbara

Ventura

Santa Barbara Channel

San Miguel Island

Santa Rosa Island

Santa Cruz Island

Anacapa Island

On Santa Cruz Island

The Ranching Recollections of
CLIFFORD McELRATH

Illustrations by John Gorham

PUBLISHED FOR THE SANTA BARBARA HISTORICAL SOCIETY BY
THE CARACTACUS CORPORATION

SANTA BARBARA, CALIFORNIA

Published for the Society by
The Caractacus Corporation
132B Harbor Way
Santa Barbara
CA 93109
(805) 963-4860
(805) 966-5237 (FAX)

Designed by Steven Brown and Krista Harris

Front cover photograph: Adobe house at the Main Ranch, Santa Cruz Island, ca. 1890. Justinian Caire had the building re-modeled in this Mediterranean style.

Back cover photograph: Main Ranch, Santa Cruz Island, 1869, the year the Santa Cruz Island Company was formed.

Note: Artistic liberties have been taken in the hand-tinting of the photographs.

Printed by Day and Night Graphics, Inc.

Library of Congress Cataloging in Publication Data

McElrath, Clifford
On Santa Cruz Island

1. California History
2. Santa Cruz Island. I. Title
Library of Congress Catalog Card Number 93-073212
ISBN 0-9634635-3-5

CONTENTS

FOREWARD

*I*n 1967, the Santa Barbara Historical Society, with Dawson's Book Shop of Los Angeles, published a volume of memoirs, *On Santa Cruz Island*. The author, Clifford McElrath, chronicles his experiences overseeing the ranching operations of the Santa Cruz Island Company from 1919 to 1921.

McElrath recalls a way of life that has more in common with the nineteenth-century era of the great rancheros than with Southern California in the twentieth century. As an example, McElrath peppers his account with a number of Spanish phrases and words not to be found in any dictionary—terms coined by the vaqueros to describe their lives spent on horseback. His recollections and "tall tales" convey a feel for the rough and tumble atmosphere of a working rancho that a purely narrative history could not.

Gracing the volume are the lyrical drawings of Santa Barbara artist John Gorham. Having grown up on a ranch near Ojai, California, Gorham successfully captures the timeless atmosphere of the ranch and the beauty of the island's landscape. The drawings wonderfully compliment McElrath's reminiscences.

The book is introduced by Dr. Carey Stanton, whose family owned most of the island from 1937 until Dr. Stanton's death in 1987. Before he died, he established the Santa Cruz Island Foundation to promote research about the Channel Islands and saw that his family's holdings on the island pass into the hands of The Nature Conservancy.

On Santa Cruz Island garnered the 1968 Western Book Award and, as only one thousand copies were printed, quickly became a collector's item. The Santa Barbara Historical Society is proud to announce, in cooperation with the Caractacus Corporation of Santa Barbara, the publication of the second edition of this long-unavailable volume. The book portrays a uniquely California culture that has disappeared from the modern scene.

MICHAEL REDMON
Librarian
Santa Barbara Historical Society

INTRODUCTION

*O*n Santa Cruz Island many things are the same as when Clifford McElrath worked here and many things are different. The office where I am writing this is still a commissary at one end and an office at the other. The high desk and the letter copying press are still here, though there is now a typewriter also. The employment records go back to 1885. These show that Clifford McElrath came to work for the island company as assistant superintendent in March 1919. Mr. Swain was superintendent then, but left in August 1919. At that time McElrath became superintendent and stayed with the island company until the end of September 1921. The Main Ranch buildings are much the same as described in this book. The large frame house of the Caire family burned in 1950. The two-story adobe house, where Mac lived on the second floor and the Swains on the first, was added onto and is now the family house. The office with small dining room next to it, kitchen, mess hall, horsebarn, saddle shop, all are largely the same. The blacksmith shop has been replaced by a shop for automotive equipment. The trasquila is now a storage shed, as no more shearing is done on this part of the island. The vineyards have long been abandoned and most of the vines removed. They are pastures now. The wineries, with all casks and wine making equipment, were gutted in the same fire that destroyed the main house. The walls were saved and new roofs put on. The upper winery is used for equipment storage and the lower is a haybarn. Most of the wagons and buggies, the surrey, and the carts were stored in the upper winery and were lost in the fire. There is still one Petaluma cart in the horse barn. The chapel is still here and whenever priests come to the island Mass is always celebrated.

The island is no longer one ranch, but two. On the east end where are Scorpion Ranch, Potato Harbor, Smugglers' Cove, the Aguaje, and other places mentioned in the book, sheep are still raised. From the Montañon and the Indian mines west it is now a cattle ranch. The cattle raised are no longer Shorthorn but Hereford, and a cattle chute is used to good advantage.

I remember well the corridas and many of the vaqueros who are mentioned. Justinian Caire II, son of Arthur Caire who hired

Mac, and Pete Olivari told me many of the same stories which are told here. The rustling, the capturing of wild cattle, making the tractor motor into a pile driver motor, trying to drive Saturno over the cliff for the motion picture company are all familiar stories to me. Pete Olivari lived and worked here until he died about five years ago. As Mac says, he was a good vaquero and all-round ranch hand, and he was a very good friend to me. Justy Caire visited the island after an absence of twenty-seven years and was pleased with what he saw.

It is amazing that in all the years that ships have been coming to the island that more pests have not been introduced. There are no rats, squirrels, rabbits, gophers, coyotes, nor poisonous snakes. Mice are native and have always been here as well as several kinds of non-poisonous snakes. Probably the only animals on the island which have been introduced since Indian times and have become naturalized are hogs, sheep, and cattle. I am familiar with the story that there once were quail on the island and that they disappeared. Near Laguna Cañon there is a Quail Cañon. In 1948 the Catalina Island variety of California Valley Quail were introduced to Santa Cruz Island and they have done extremely well.

In a strong northeaster on December 6, 1960, the *Santa Cruz* parted her mooring chain in Prisoners' Harbor and was totally destroyed on the rocks on the west side of the harbor. The *Santa Cruz* was built by Matthew Turner in Benicia, California, in 1893. Justinian Caire had her built for the Santa Cruz Island Company. She was used only to serve Santa Cruz Island and occasionally others of the Channel Islands.

This book is a charming remembrance of life on Santa Cruz Island nearly fifty years ago. It is a small part of California history well worth preserving. How regrettable that more of "los viejos" do not record their memories.

CAREY STANTON

Main Ranch, Santa Cruz Island
April 10, 1967

SANTA CRUZ ISLAND

*T*he first time that I saw Santa Cruz Island was when I visited my sister and her husband, Dr. Ben Bakewell, in Santa Barbara. This was shortly after I was discharged from the Army following World War I. The large island about twenty miles to the south intrigued my imagination. Sometimes it was plainly visible and sometimes only dimly seen with its higher peaks shrouded in clouds or fog.

I asked many questions about it but no one seemed to know much. "Oh yes, it is one big ranch where they raise cattle and sheep and make some wine." That was about all anyone I talked to knew. In fact, no one seemed very much interested. By a curious chain of events, too long to narrate here, I was hired by Mr. Arthur Caire, one of the owners, to go down there in charge of the cattle. My job was what was known on most large ranches

1

as cattle boss. I was given the much fancier title of assistant superintendent.

I crossed from Santa Barbara to the island on the *Santa Cruz,* a sturdy two-masted schooner sixty feet long.[1] Before becoming the property of the Santa Cruz Island Company, she had been an icebreaker in the Arctic and was very well built. The *Santa Cruz* was equipped with both sails and an engine. When the wind was right, she made as good or better time under sail as she did with her engine.

The *Santa Cruz* looked like a typical South Sea island trader when under sail and heeled over to the breeze. Anchored in a cove with sails furled and with the hills and headlands as a background, she looked more than ever like something lifted bodily from a South Seas novel. On several occasions, moving picture companies used her as a background for South Sea island scenes.

Although it is getting ahead of my story, I want to insert an incident that happened several months after I arrived on the island. One of the companies was making pictures, some of them using the *Santa Cruz* as background. The script called for the hero or the villain, I am not sure which, to climb the ratlines to the top of the mast, during which climb a knife whizzed past his ear and stuck quivering in the mast. After reaching the top, he was to hook his toes around the $5/8$th cable that stretched between the two masts and dive out over the edge or gunwales of the ship and escape by swimming ashore.

There was only one drawback. They had not brought anyone with them capable of the feat or even willing to try it. The masts reached skyward about sixty or sixty-five feet from the deck and the cable was about five feet from the tip of the masts.

Somehow they learned that there was a young man named Tony at the Main Ranch who could probably do what they wanted, so the director and a couple of assistants talked the caretaker out of his Petaluma cart and arrived at the ranch all in a sweat and demanding to see Tony. Tony was a clean-cut, good looking young California Spaniard in the early twenties. At the time, he was taking the bull cook's place, the latter having gone to Santa Barbara on his annual two-week spree.

After they explained what they wanted, Tony said, "Yes, I can do it." Then after a little more haggling, they agreed on what they would pay him. They then demanded that he return with them at once, but I guess Tony had a bit of the prima donna in him because he said he would come down after lunch, when he had finished washing the dishes; and nothing could move him. So the entire company, stars and all, sat around and waited for Tony. I went down to see the show.

When Tony finally arrived, they fixed him up in a loincloth, explained what he was to do, and Tony went up the ratlines like a monkey. When he reached the top, he poised for a moment, standing on the cable and holding to the mast with one hand, gauging the breeze and catching the roll of the boat. When the roll was just right, he gave a spring and dove out, missing the gunwales by a wide margin in as pretty a dive as I ever saw performed by a professional. He then swam ashore, put on his clothes, collected his pay, and returned to the ranch to prepare the vegetables for the men's supper.

Tony was an avid hunter. He spent most of his spare time hunting wild boars. He was a crack shot with a rifle but seldom used one. He preferred to hunt with a dog and a home-made lance, always on foot. This took some nimble footwork if the dog bayed a big, old boar amongst rocks, cactus, and brush.

But to get back to that first crossing. The crew of the *Santa Cruz* consisted of three men. There was Captain Olivari, a picturesque old deep-water sailor who had been around the world several times and sailed the seven seas on windjammers. His son, Pete, was a good sailor and was also a good vaquero. He worked part of the time with the cattle and took time off from sailing to act as mayordomo of the corridas or sheep roundups. He was an all around, good, ranch hand. The third man at that time was Eduardo, a Barbareño or Santa Barbara Spaniard, with the usual mixture of Indian. He was a man about sixty years old.

The day I crossed over to the island, Eduardo was the helmman. I sat in the stern chatting with him. One of his first questions was to ask me if I had been in the Army. On my answering in the affirmative he replied, "I served my country for fifteen years in the cavalry. I was one of Teddy's Rough Riders and was with him at San Juan Hill. After that I was with the regular cavalry during the Philippine Insurrection." He then went on to tell me about his experiences in the Philippines. He had all of the army lingo and was very convincing. I had no reason to disbelieve him.

After we landed, I was driving to the Main Ranch with Mr. Swain, the superintendent. We were riding in an old time, two wheeled Petaluma cart drawn by one horse. As we jogged along I remarked, "That is an interesting old boy on the schooner. The one called Eduardo."

"What did he tell you?" asked Mr. Swain. I then recounted what I had been told. Mr. Swain laughed and then was silent for a short space of time. Then he looked at me with a grin and said, "The only time he ever served his country was when he served time in San Quentin for slipping a knife between another Spanish boy's ribs." Such was my introduction to the island and to one of a number of characters I was to meet during the years it was to be my home.

I was assigned to a room on the second floor of the adobe house in which the superintendent and his wife made their home. My room had two windows. It was reached by an outside stairway with a roofless porch about four feet square at the top of the stairs, the porch being surrounded by a wrought-iron railing all forged out by hand on the island. The balustrade to the stairs was the same. In the room was a bed with mattress and a pillow; I had my own sheets, pillow cases, and blankets. There were a couple of straight-backed chairs, a bureau of sorts, and a curtained-off section to hang my clothes in. There was also an old styled marble-topped washstand on top of which was a pitcher of cold water, a wash bowl, a tumbler, and a soap dish. On the floor was a bucket or slop jar, as they were called, for dirty water. A small table and a kerosene lamp completed the furnishings.

Other conveniences were on a hillside several hundred feet away. The bull cook swept my room, kept my water pitcher full, and emptied the slop bucket. He also did my washing but no ironing. When I wanted a hot bath, I carried a pitcher of hot water from the kitchen and took a sponge bath.

I had my own dining room in one end of the office building, a few steps from the kitchen, where my meals were served by the same bull cook. Cattle buyers and others who visited the island ate with me, as did Mr. Caire when he visited the island without his family.

The office was about twenty-four feet long and about fourteen feet wide. One half of it was a combination store and commissary. We kept a few staple articles such as knives, jeans, jumpers, underwear, soap, cartridges, and Toscano cigars, which the men could purchase and have charged against their accounts. The other half was the office.

The office furniture was a couple of chairs, a couple of high stools, and two high desks that it was necessary to stand up to when writing unless you sat on one of the high stools. There was no such thing as a typewriter; all correspondence was in longhand. We wrote with copying ink, using an ordinary pen. One then put the letter on a second sheet with a dry blotter as I remember under it and a damp blotter on top, or perhaps it was the other way around. The whole works was then put into the copying press, a machine with two flat iron faces and a large screw and handle like a wine press. You then screwed down to get pressure on the paper, left the letter in the press for a few minutes and out came a fairly good copy on very thin paper that had to be read from the back side of the sheet. I wish I had that old copying press! It had been a museum piece for many years before I ever saw it and would rate with an old spinning wheel today.

I arrived on the island on a Saturday afternoon. As no one worked on Sunday excepting the cook and the stableman, I spent the day exploring on foot around the Main Ranch. It was an interesting day.

The buildings with two exceptions were located on the south side of and about the center of the large interior valley. There was a fairly large one-story frame house that the owners and their families occupied when they visited the island. The superintendent's house was a well-built two-story adobe with a fireplace in the living room, the office a long, low frame building, and the kitchen and men's dining room a long one-story adobe. In front of the kitchen was an old-style brick oven that looked like a giant beehive. It was no longer used as they had put more modern ovens in the kitchen. Since both ovens were fired by wood I could never quite see the reason. The old-style brick ovens were still used at the other ranches and I always thought the bread made in them was much better. Maybe it was my imagination.

The horse barn was a good-looking, well-built brick building with stalls and the stableman's room on the first floor and a large hayloft above. The bricks for this building and several other brick buildings at the ranch had all been moulded from red clay and burned in a kiln on a nearby hillside. They were as well made as any bricks one might get from a brickyard on the mainland.

On either side of the horse barn were the sillería or saddle and harness shop, where repairs were made to saddles and harness, and the blacksmith shop. We had our own saddle and harness maker, also a blacksmith who was a genius as a mechanic, Enrique Lopes. He could do all the repair work and maintenance on wagons, plows, etc., could forge out as good a pair of pruning shears as one could buy in a hardware store, or could clean and repair a fine watch without even a magnifying glass such as watchmakers use. I have never been sure, however, whether he could not or just would not shoe a horse.

Enrique was a large powerful man and truly fit the description of "a strong silent man." I learned as time went on that when I met him in the yard in the morning and said, "Buenos días, Enrique," if he answered me with only a grunt everything was alright. If he answered "Buenos días, patrón," I knew that he had gotten hold of some liquor and was drunk enough to be real talkative for him. This only happened once or twice a year.

There were other buildings such as the trasquila, long semi-open sheds where the sheep were sheared, the matanza or slaughter house, and two bunk houses, one a frame building and the other adobe. Trasquila comes from the Spanish word, trasquilar, meaning to shear.

There was the winery, a large two-story brick building. It was made of island-burned bricks and built by old country artisans to last forever. Here wine made from the grapes grown on several hundred adjoining acres was made and stored in vats and tanks up to five thousand gallons each. These tanks, I was told, had all been made on the island of oak wood imported from the mainland. The hoops and staves all shaped and fitted by hand. They were beautiful specimens of craftsmanship.

Across the valley from the ranch buildings, situated in a corner of the vineyard, was the cantina vieja or old winery. This was the first winery built on the island and was still in use for storing wine for use on the island. It was a board and batten building built on a limestone foundation. The men were given a daily ration of a small bottle of piquette or watered down wine with their lunch and evening meal.

Nearby was a small brick Catholic chapel complete with altar. Once a year when the Caire families were visiting the island during the summer months a padre would come from Santa Barbara and hold services for the family and any of the men who cared to attend.

Directly opposite the ranch yard the stream had through the ages cut its way through the mountains and formed the gorge that led to Prisoners' Harbor and the ocean. It was along the floor of the canyon that the road to the harbor wound. Directly below the ranch the floor of the canyon was not over fifty feet wide with hills rising almost perpendicularly to a height of one thousand to twelve hundred feet. It then widened out to a rocky sandy river bed almost a half mile in width.

The road was practically level. In the three miles from the harbor there was a difference in elevation of only about fifty feet. There were many beautiful live oak trees on the hillsides directly below the ranch and also on the alluvial fans at the foot of the hills.

The stream which flowed under ground from Portezuela, three miles to the west, rose to the surface at the Main Ranch and ran as a fair-sized stream for about a quarter of a mile when it went underground until it reached the harbor, where it again came to the surface in a small lagoon which supplied water for livestock. It had also supplied water for a large Indian village if one can judge by the size of the shell mound at that point. On the bank just below the ranch yard was a fine spring of clear soft water from which we used to carry drinking water in a pitcher. On the stream itself each year a pair of woodducks raised their brood, becoming quite tame. No doubt some of the men looked at them with the idea of roast duck in mind but I let it be known in simple and maybe rather direct language that if anyone ate those ducks it would be the last meal he would eat until he reached Santa Barbara, so they were never molested.

Of course I did not learn all of the above facts in a single day's exploring. Much of it is the accumulation of information and observations over the time I spent on the island. Not being a professional writer I take this opportunity to ask my readers to bear with the fact that my writing does not always have perfect continuity, in addition to errors in grammar and punctuation.

The following day Mr. Swain, Cuate Espinoza, an old California vaquero who had spent a large part of his life on the island, and I started riding so that I could get acquainted with the country. That day we rode to Pelican Bay. Much of the trail from Prisoners' Harbor to Pelican Bay was through a forest of Monterey pines. At Pelican Bay was a small resort run by Ira Eaton, the captain of the *Sea Wolf,* a small boat in which he took fishing parties and guests to his resort. He leased the ground from the island company.

From there we climbed a steep cuchillo or ridge to the summit and from there descended another cuchillo to Portezuela and Buena Vista and from there home. This took the better part of a day.

The following day we rode to the Christy Ranch. Mr. Swain not wanting to leave his wife alone, returned home that afternoon and Cuate and I stayed at the Christy for a few days to look the cattle over and let me get acquainted with that part of the island.

I was riding a very good tordilla, named Gracia. A tordilla is a grey or more properly white mare with numerous brown hairs giving her a speckled appearance. Gracia was no longer young and by this time she was, after several long days in rough country, commencing to gaunt up and drag her feet. I did everything I could to make it easy for her but she needed a few days rest.

While riding the range out of the Christy we encountered a band of good-looking horses, some of them yearlings but most of them mature horses weighing from one thousand to eleven hundred pounds. They were wild and spooky and took off over the low hills as soon almost as they saw us. I asked Cuate about them and he told me that they ranged in age up to about eight years and that none of them had ever felt a rope or been corraled since they were cut as yearlings. Already from a distance I had made up my mind which ones I would like to have in my string.

On returning to the Main Ranch I asked Mr. Swain about them. Knowing that we were short of good horses I asked why we didn't break them. His reply was short and to the point. "Because I have not found anyone who would tackle the job." Maybe it was because during my teens I had ridden a number of buckers, maybe it was because of my desire to have some of those horses in my string and maybe it was just the confidence of youth that made me say, "I'll break them for you." After a little dickering it was agreed that I would break them for a small, very small, raise in salary and the privilege of taking my pick of the horses. So I added the title of bronc rider or jinete, as the Spanish called it, to my title of assistant superintendent.

The word quickly spread that I was the new jinete. The men were naturally curious as to when I was going to start. Some volunteered advice such as "Cuidado, son muy reparosos," meaning "Be careful. They are bad buckers." They were curious to see whether I really was "un jinete."

They had an exhibition of my skill or lack of it sooner than any of us expected. In order to let my mare, Gracia, have a few days rest Mr. Swain pointed out a good-looking bay gelding named Boy and told me I could use him for a change off. He warned me that if I put my feet forward as though I was going to spur him in the shoulders or let my cinch get loose going down hill I was in for a ride. Otherwise he said Boy was a first class cow horse.

As soon as I was well out of sight of the ranch I selected a clear flat area and took down my jaquima rope so that if I got piled my horse wouldn't get away. Then I hooked both spurs in his shoulders. Some outfits have bad buckers and some don't. I wanted to find out what the island horses were like. Boy immediately went into action. He did not buck hard. In fact he only crow-hopped a few jumps and quit when I took my spurs off his shoulders. I patted him on the neck and thought to myself, "If that is what they call a bucker they probably have a fairly gentle strain of horses and I shouldn't have too much trouble."

All of the vineyards not having been plowed as yet it was the practice to turn the horses loose in them at night to take advantage of the lush green grass and save hay, which was getting low. We kept a saddle horse in the corral at night to use in driving the others in the morning.

I kept Boy in that night and the next morning put the saddle on him before breakfast so as not to lose time in getting the horses in. Right after breakfast I got on him without tightening the saddle. Maybe I forgot but then I have never been one of those riders who tries to cut his horse in two with the cinch, just tight enough so that the saddle won't slip.

We climbed the hill and got the herd started. They were feeling frisky with their bellies full of grass and knew where they were going so the whole bunch started off at a lope along the hillside with me loping along behind them. There was a rather steep vineyard road leading down to the gate into the ranch yard. The herd turned down the road with me right behind them.

How it happened I am not sure. I guess Boy just jumped out from under me. Anyway I landed on my back in a freshly pruned grapevine almost like a cradle except that those newly-pruned stubs made it different from any cradle I ever knew. They took most of my shirt and a lot of hide off my back with it. My head was higher than my feet and I could see Boy going down the hill. He wasn't doing any crow-hopping. He was really pouring on the coal. I could almost hear him say, "Sucker! I sure fooled you into thinking I was an easy horse to ride."

The entire ranch force had a grandstand seat to see the new bronc rider piled higher than a kite. As I walked by a couple of the men in the ranch yard I heard one say in Spanish, "They say he is the new bronc rider," and they both laughed. It was rather embarrassing and I was mad. However I was madder at Boy than I was at them. I caught him and got on and jabbed both spurs into his shoulders at the same time hitting him a crack with my romal. Three or four half hearted bucks were all I could get out of him. He worked strictly on the principle of surprise.

When someone asked me how I had come to be thrown I used my stock excuse in similar situations, "I wasn't good enough to stay on." This caused a laugh; plus the fact that I had gotten on without changing my shirt or washing the blood off my back and tried to make him buck, it resulted in my being accepted as jinete de verdad, a real bronc rider. I never let Boy catch me by surprise again although he tried. As I got to know the men a lot of them admitted that Boy had unloaded them too.

There followed days of riding. I spent several days at the Scorpion Ranch at the east end of the island. From there I rode to the Aguaje, Smugglers' Cove, Potato Harbor, Mielquieres, and what we called the Indian Territory. This was a large area stretching from the Aguaje to the Sur Ranch on the south side of the island. There was no water, not even a spring, from the Aguaje to the Sur. The Indian Territory got its name from the small caves in the chalk rock hills, the walls and ceilings of which were blackened by smoke. In front of each cave were deposits of shells hardly large enough to be called a shell mound or kitchen midden. It is hard to believe that Indians lived so far from water. The size of the shell deposits, some of them not over two or three inches thick, showed that there had been no long-continued habitations in or around the caves. They may have been just overnight campsites but were more probably hideouts from marauding Aleuts or soldiers from the missions seeking neophytes. I have found the same small shell deposits on the highest ridges cleverly concealed by thickets of manzanita which could only be explained as places of concealment.

My next job was breaking horses. At the Christy Ranch there was a beautiful sandy beach over a mile long. I thought the beach would be a good place to ride the broncs. They would tire quickly, couldn't buck too hard, and it would be a soft landing spot if I were thrown.

My first horse was a big blue roan. I saddled him in the corral and my hazer worked him down to the beach. He was not yet halter-broken. I mounted him and with the help of my hazer rode him the length of the beach and back. He made no attempt to buck even when I spurred him so I started up to the corral to saddle another. As soon as that horse felt solid ground under his feet he bogged his head and went to bucking. That was a bad start. If a horse starts out by going along quietly the first time he is ridden and then starts bucking when you least expect it he is liable to carry the habit the rest of his life. It is no fun to have a horse start bucking in the middle of a bunch of trees or brush or on a steep rocky hillside. That is just what that big moro did. You could never trust him even when he seemed tired out. He was the first and last horse that I ever broke on a beach or in sand. The rest of them I rode in the big corral for a couple of days, then around the floor of the valley for a few days, finally winding up with a couple of full days' rides. By that time they were usually tired enough so that they had lost the desire to throw the rider off and I could turn them over to other riders to use steadily every day. Hard work day after day and they soon tamed down. Many of the horses broken by "broncing them out" were never completely tame. After being turned out for a rest they bucked as hard as ever the first couple of days when put back to work. Some of the riders would ride them but more often the jinete had to take them on for a couple of days. Of course some of the horses never bucked.

Most green horses do not buck too hard. They buck a few jumps and then run giving an occasional buck or two as they run. This soon tires them and the rider can then start pulling them around and teaching them to obey the jaquima.

So much for my first few weeks on the island. About this time the corridas or sheep roundups began, followed by the rounding up and branding of the cattle. These are whole chapters in themselves so at this point I am going to try to give a brief description of the island and some of its outstanding features.

Santa Cruz is the largest of the Channel Islands. It is located about twenty miles south of Santa Barbara and has an area of about sixty-four thousand acres. The island is about twenty miles in length and varies from two or three miles to twelve miles in width. It is mountainous; the highest peak Picacho Diablo, rises to over nineteen hundred feet and is occasionally covered with snow for a few days at a time in winter. The main mountain chain, running east and west, reaches an altitude of from one thousand to twelve hundred feet, possibly a little higher in places.[2]

This mountain chain splits into two ridges about the center of the island. These continue on to the west end of the island like a giant pair of legs. A few miles from the east end there is a high volcanic ridge that crosses the island at right angles to the main ridge, making a perfect cross. Perhaps this is the reason for the name of the island, Santa Cruz.[3] One could also carry on the analogy of the two legs and call this ridge the arms.

In the central valley formed by the two mountain chains lies the Main Ranch with its fields and vineyards. Four miles to the east from the Main Ranch was the Sur Ranch, with a good adobe house and a running stream. This ranch had been abandoned for some years when I went to the island.

Several miles west of the Main Ranch the road to the Christy Ranch ascends a steep grade to Portezuela and Buena Vista. This is an upland valley between the same mountain ridges. Portezuela is the Spanish word for a relatively flat upland valley. At Portezuela was an old half-adobe and half-log cabin whose history I never learned. We used it as a cook house when we had a hay crew camped there. At Buena Vista the road again descended through a steep canyon to the valley that led on to the Christy Ranch.

At the Christy was a good two-story adobe in which the foreman and his wife lived—also the dining room where the men ate. There were also the horse barn and trasquila, corrals, etc., and adobe bunk house. The bunk house was said to be the oldest building on the island. No one knew just how old or who had built it. It contained one long room and on the wall at the north end of the room was a religious painting, a cross, etc., that was said to have been painted by the original builder. The colors were as bright and clear as the day it was painted. They were probably natural pigments from plants or colored earth.

There were Indian shell mounds at the mouth of almost every canyon or valley. They varied greatly in size and many of them had been badly or almost entirely eroded away by stream action during the winter freshets. Several of the largest, however, were still almost intact. The largest and best specimen was about two or three miles from the Christy Ranch. One reason was that it was not located on a stream bank; another was that the nearest point at which boats could land was Forney's Cove, several miles distant over rough, rocky, cactus-grown land cut by steep gullies. This would have discouraged curio hunters even if they had known of its existence. The third and most important reason was that the Spanish vaqueros were very superstitious about it. "It was the home of the king of the Indians, señor, and any one who goes there or disturbs it will have very bad luck. Many years ago a man went there looking for pedronales (arrowheads) and he died in less than six months." They passed the superstition on to the Italian farm hands and no one would go closer than a quarter of a mile. They thought I was very brave or more likely foolhardy because when gathering cattle or otherwise looking them over I would ride over to the mound. It gave me a chance to look it over. It had a definite pattern of whale ribs laid on the top of the mound. I never saw this anywhere else. I confess I did nothing to try to cure their superstition. I thought it would be a nice thing to keep that mound as it was. I explained my own bravado by telling them that an old woman had put a charm on me when I was very young that protected me from evil spirits. I wasn't really lying. My mother had taught me when very young not to be superstitious or afraid of the dark. What better charm could one have?

While talking of Indian inhabitants of the island before the somewhat doubtful blessings of being converted and civilized overtook them, I want to mention the Indian Mines, Minas de los Indios as we called them. These were located on the northwest shoulder of the Montagnon. They were holes roughly ten to twenty feet in diameter and from four to six feet deep. They had been laboriously dug out of the volcanic rock with stone and wooden implements to get at the veins of white flint.[4] Around their edges were innumerable chips and pieces of arrowheads broken in the process of making them. I have read that most of the white flint arrowheads found on the mainland—and not very many are found—came from Santa Cruz Island. They were an important article of commerce with the Indians on the mainland and the other islands.

There are numerous running streams on the island, between fifteen and twenty all told. These streams rise in the high hills, run short distances, and sink underground. They may appear and disappear several times on their trip to the sea. None of them, however, actually reach the sea, except during infrequent winter storms. A few of the larger ones appear close to the ocean in the form of fresh or brackish lagoons. Most of the streams have varying amounts of alkali but are sufficiently fresh to furnish water for livestock and I have drunk from all of them when thirsty.

There are also a number of springs. Some of them are very good water.

There are a number of good harbors. All of them are exposed to certain winds and when these particular winds come up suddenly any boat anchored in that particular harbor has to get out in a hurry. Prisoners' Harbor is perhaps the best of all but when one of the infrequent northeasters starts it is a case of run for Potato Harbor even if it is the middle of the night.

A few miles west of Prisoners' Harbor is the so-called Painted Cave. This is washed out of the cliffs by the ocean. The opening is about twenty or thirty feet in diameter and at low tide if the surf is not running too high one can enter in a skiff. How far back it runs I don't think anyone knows unless divers have explored it since I was there. A couple of us were able to get into the cave for a distance of maybe two or three hundred feet. At that point the roof was too low to go any farther. That day there were a number of sea lions resting on the ledges beside the water. Between their barking and splashing and the echo it all set up inside the cave they made it sound like a madhouse as they swam under our boat and around it on the way to the open sea. As to the name Painted Cave, that is probably poetic license. I saw no evidence of highly colored rock formations such as the name suggests—just the usual grays and browns that one would expect in a wave-washed cave.

As to the native trees, shrubs, and grasses: they are about the same as on the mainland. The grasses were wild oats, foxtail, bronco grass, burr clover, and alfileria. The brush was manzanita and chapparal. The native trees were live oak, Monterey pine, wild cherry or islay, a few cottonwoods, willow, and palo fierro. Groves of eucalyptus had been planted at several places and were used as piling for the wharf and for firewood.

As to the palo fierro, I was told that this particular species exists only in three places: Santa Cruz Island, in some canyons back of San Diego, and in New Zealand. As to the truth of this I cannot say.[5] There are only a few small clumps on the island. They are a very pretty deciduous tree about twenty-five or thirty feet tall with trunk not over five or six inches in diameter.

The climate of the island varies greatly depending on exposure to the sea, etc. At the Main Ranch we had frost in winter, while at the Scorpion Ranch, fourteen miles away, there would still be ripe tomatoes on the vines. In summer it would get hot at the Main Ranch and the Christy Ranch would be cold, foggy, and windy. The fall and winter at the Christy were usually clear and balmy with very little wind.

As to the birds and native animals of the island there have undoubtedly been scientific articles written about them. I don't even know their Latin names. But as a riding cowboy who spent many hours and covered many miles with no other companion but my horse and the birds and animals around me I came to know their habits, their good traits and bad ones, and sometimes amusing ones. I will try to tell something about them in the following chapter.

Notes:

1. See introduction for story of the origin of the schooner, *Santa Cruz*.

2. McElrath's figures are a little off here. The island is about twenty-two miles long and varies from two to six miles in width for a total area of sixty-two thousand acres. Picacho Diablo is 2,434 feet high.

3. The island was named during the Gaspar de Portolá expedition in 1769, when a walking staff topped by a cross was lost by one of the expedition's priests and was returned by an Indian.

4. Arrowheads were made of chert, a type of quartz. It was often very light in color.

5. This type of ironwood is also found on the islands of San Clemente and Santa Rosa.

BIRDS AND ANIMALS OF
SANTA CRUZ ISLAND

$\mathcal{T}$he only strictly native animals on the island were numerous small red foxes and a few civet cats. A civet cat is a small species of skunk. The foxes were smaller and tamer than the mainland members of the fox family. Often they would just sit and watch one ride by without seeking cover. The civet cats were either very scarce or else, being night prowlers, we did not see them very often. I don't remember seeing more than three or four in all the time that I spent on the island. One I remember very well.[1]

One summer when the Caire families were visiting the island they had a Chinese cook. There were still some of the old time Chinese that spoke pidgin English. He was one of them.

I do not recall his name but he managed to catch a civet cat in a box trap. Then by what can be ascribed only to Celestial good luck he managed to transfer the cat to a flimsy wire cage about the size of a bird cage—all this without getting sprayed by said cat.

I was taking a trip to Santa Barbara on the schooner, as were a couple of the men. I was all dressed up in my store clothes and had my suitcase with me so I was riding to the harbor in a Petaluma cart instead of on horseback. The two men were riding with me.

As we were about to leave the ranch the cook approached carrying the cage with the civet cat in it in one hand and between his thumb and forefinger of the other hand he held a twenty-five cent piece.

When he got close to the cart he said to me, "You likee catchee two bittee? You takee skunk my flend in Santa Baba."

My reply was "Get away from here with that skunk." He did not move until he had made the same offer to the other two men and been turned down. He then turned away muttering in Chinese but with Oriental shrewdness he did not raise his original offer of "two bittee." What became of the civet cat I never knew. Probably the cook turned him loose.

When I was on the island there were no rats, mice, gophers, squirrels, rabbits, or coyotes. There was no evidence that there ever had been any. Neither were there any snakes.[2] Of course it was inevitable that some rats and mice would get over in bales or boxes and maybe some just hitch-hiked over on boats. Because of this we kept a couple of cats around the bodega or warehouse at the harbor and a couple at the Main Ranch. If any rats or mice got by the cats they still had foxes, civet cats, crows, and a few hawks and owls to contend with. I don't think any ever survived to start a second generation.

As to birds, there were numerous bald eagles, great numbers of large crows—they may have been ravens—fish hawks, doves, some blue jays, and the general run of small birds such as linnets, sparrows, robins, etc. I was told that a year or two before I went to the island the quail which had existed in great numbers either took sick and all died off or they had migrated to other parts. While I was there I never saw one.

At the west end of the island we had several flocks of a small bird a little larger than a sparrow that we called a parakeet. They were of a dull brown color and had the typical bill of a parakeet. They stayed in an area of about six hundred acres of cactus and low brush and I never saw them outside this particular area. I have read that there are no parakeets north of southern Texas and these may not have been true parakeets. I have never seen them anywhere else and have wondered sometimes if it might not be a stray colony that came north and decided to settle permanently. It is hard to figure out how a flock of tropical birds would decide to settle on the most windswept, cold, and inhospitable portion of the island as a permanent home.

The bald eagles were very numerous and killed many lambs. I never knew one to take a lamb over a few days old. They would take a small lamb to the top of a tree or crag and, holding it in their claws, peel the skin off very much as we would a banana, eat the lamb, and drop the skin, head, and feet at the foot of the tree or crag. Often we would find many small skins at the foot of one of their favorite perches.

Their method of getting a fish dinner was interesting. An eagle would perch on a tall tree or rock close to the shore and wait. Sooner or later a fish hawk would come along. The hawk would dive and almost always come up with a fish in his talons. Mr. Eagle would wait until the hawk was high above the water and then dive at him with a piercing scream. The hawk would drop the fish in terror and take off. The eagle would dive, catch the fish in midair and retire to his tree to enjoy his hi-jacked dinner. Mostly however the eagles were carrion eaters. I have seen as many as a half dozen tearing at and gorging themselves on a dead animal while the crows hopped around the outskirts waiting for their chance.

It was always interesting and amusing to watch a flock of pelicans when they followed a school of fish into the harbor or some cove late in the afternoon. As they circled and banked a few feet above the water the setting sun would shine on the underside of their wings, turning them to a delicate pink.

Suddenly a pelican would dive straight down and come up with a fish in his beak. If the fish was crosswise with the head sticking out of one side and the tail sticking out of the other, immediately the pelican would be surrounded by several sea gulls trying to get the fish away from him. They usually succeeded. There were some pelicans that I assumed to be older, smarter birds. They would catch a fish and keep their bills under water almost up to their eyes until they had the fish safely in the pouch under their bills. They looked so wise, almost like a judge or a professor. I could almost imagine that I could see them roll their eyes at the gulls as they said "Get lost." Maybe they did both.

The crows were the most ornery, mean, audacious, intelligent, and interesting of all the birds. There were a number of them who made the Main Ranch their hangout. Hangout is the only word that fits the place where such a bunch of thieves and cutthroats made their home. They were probably attracted by the hides hanging on the fence around the matanza to dry and by the pens where from six to a dozen hogs were fed.

The stableman, Abelino Lugo, a dour old California Spaniard who seemed to croak with the voice of doom when he spoke, would look at the crows and remark half to himself, "Son las almas de los Indios. Vuelven a molestar a los blancos" (They are the souls of the Indians. They have returned to pester the white people). After I had been on the island for a while I more than half way believed he was right.

Occasionally when I thought there were too many of them, that they were getting too cocky, or maybe I was just tired of their cawing, I would take my shotgun, walk down towards the matanza and give them a bad time. Some would fly up and perch in the tall eucalyptus trees and others would gather in a clear spot on the hillside about a quarter of a mile away but every one of them would spend the next half hour telling me what they thought of me and all my relatives.

After bombarding the crows and killing two or three of them I could not repeat the performance for two or three weeks. The instant I stepped out of a door with a gun some crow would give the alarm and they would all take off. Unbelievable as it may sound I could go out with a stick, a broom, or a shovel and approach to within twenty feet of where they were sitting on the fence, picking bits of meat off the drying hides, and none of them would pay any more attention to me than to hop over to another fence a few feet away, cocking his head on one side and maybe giving a derisive caw.

There was one long, very windy ridge that I often rode along on my way to and from the Scorpion Ranch. It was part of the trail between the Montagnon and Campo Chino. It followed the backbone of the island and was open to the full force of the winds whether they were from the northwest in summer or the southeast in winter.

Along this trail I was always accompanied by one or two crows, seldom more. They would fly about one hundred feet in front of me usually not more than five or six feet off the ground. Suddenly catching an updraft one or both would shoot almost straight up to a height of one hundred feet or more then swoop out over one of the canyons, hold themselves stationary against the wind for a couple of seconds, and then with a long graceful sideways glide sweep back to their original position in front of me. They would vary this sometimes by looping the loop or sudden sideslips all with the skill and cocksureness of born showoffs.

If I had an old or mature dog with me the crows paid him no attention. But if I had a pup or a young dog then the crows had a field day. They would hover over him, rising easily and gracefully just out of reach of his frenzied leaps all the time cawing and teasing him until the poor pup was completely worn out or had learned his lesson—that he couldn't catch a crow on the wing.

Often if the wind was stronger than usual the crows would carry a rock about the size of an egg in their claws. It was undoubtedly for ballast. I never saw them drop it. When the trail dropped down from the ridge to the Campo Chino flats they would desert me. It was no fun when they did not have the wind with its up and down drafts to help them put on their act.

The black devils could also be fiends. Let a ewe and her newborn lamb become isolated and two crows would attack them. One crow would divert the ewe by dancing in front of her while the other attacked the lamb trying to pick its eyes out. When the ewe rushed at the attacking bird he would dance off in front of her and his partner took up the role of attacker. Ultimately they would succeed, the lamb would die, and the crows had their ill-gotten meal.

I never watched this event through to its finish. I rushed at them with my horse, pelted them with rocks or occasionally took a shot at them with my Colt .45. I have never enjoyed killing for the sake of killing but I was always glad when I was lucky enough to get one of those murderous devils.

During the winter months when most of the cattle and sheep were thin it was sometimes a problem to get meat that was anything but skin and bones. Some of the sheep, however, were always fairly fat. They were the wildest of the sheep and probably kept fat on browse in the high hills, only coming down to the valley for water or a change of diet. They were long tailed or "coludos," sheep that had never been corraled.

When one jumped a bunch of sheep it was easy to tell the fat ones or at least those that were not too thin to eat. The tails of the thin ones flopped up and down like a wet rag. The tails of the fat ones whirled round and round in a circle as they ran. Of course being stronger they were also in the lead.

When we needed meat several of us on good horses would start up the valley followed by a wagon with high sides. When we jumped a bunch of sheep feeding on one of the flats we would start after them. Each of us would pick out one that seemed fairly fat and if luck was with us we would rope and hogtie our sheep before it got to the brush. The wagon following along would pick it up, take the piggin string off its legs, and put it in the wagon. After we had collected from a dozen to twenty sheep we would return to the ranch, put them in a corral with feed and water, and the ranch had a meat supply for a while.

I remember the first sheep I caught. I jumped off my horse and tied all four legs. Pete Olivari, who was later to become superintendent of the island for a number of years, was with us that day. He stopped his horse and told me, "Meester, you must leave one front foot loose." I asked him why and he told me, "Eef you tie all hees feet the cuervos (crows) gon peek hees eyes out before the wagon she get here." I learned this to be true. If you did not leave one foot free for protection whether it be sheep, calf, or any other animal the crows would pick its eyes out as soon as you turned your back.

"Son las almas de los Indios." Ya lo creo, I believe it.

The other animals on the island were horses, cattle, sheep, and wild hogs. Of course none of these were native and will be written about in following chapters. Oh, yes, contrary to popular belief that there are a lot of wild goats on the island there were possibly two wild goats on the entire island.

When I first started riding Mr. Swain told me that two billy goats that were used in the corrals to help with the sheep had escaped two years previous. They had never been able to catch them and they had disrupted several corridas by leading the sheep into rough, inaccessible country. He told me to try to spot them and then come back and get a rifle and shoot them. Mr. Swain never allowed any riders to carry guns for reasons that I will give in a later chapter.

It was a couple of years later when I had become superintendent and had lifted the ban on riders' going armed that four of us saw one of the goats sunning himself just about sunset on a high peak. We worked around until there was one of us on each side of the peak. The goat dashed down the side where Cuate Espinoza was stationed and Cuate got him.

He was an angora goat with beautiful long hair but I never saw any animal so matted with burrs, fox-tail, and cactus, besides manure and twigs. Cuate took one look at the hide and said he did not want it. He was only interested in the meat for jerky. No one else wanted it so I took the hide. I wanted to try an experiment.

I had heard that the best way to clean a dirty sheep or goat skin was to tow it behind a boat in salt water. I towed that hide all the way to Santa Barbara behind the *Santa Cruz*. It worked. I never saw a cleaner more beautiful hide. It was not only clean but all the hair looked like it had been combed and combed—not a snarl or a tangle left in it. I then sent it away and had it tanned. It was a beauty.

As far as I know nothing was ever seen of the second goat. Maybe some fisherman or yachtsman got him.

Notes:

1. There actually are four terrestrial mammals native to the island: the western harvest mouse, the deer mouse, the island fox, and the spotted skunk.

2. There are two species of snake on Santa Cruz Island. For a brief discussion of the types of plants and animals found on the Channel Islands, see Marla Daily, *California's Channel Islands 1001 Questions Answered* (Santa Barbara: McNally and Loftin, 1987).

C ORRIDAS

_L_as corridas were the roundup of semi-wild sheep for shearing, docking the lambs, etc. We used from twenty to twenty-five vaqueros and a large remuda of horses. As to the vaqueros, they were old time Californios and some of the best vaqueros I have ever known. Most of them were middle-aged or older, some real old. About all of them have gone to that big ranch up in the sky and with them went a great breed of horsemen and cowboys.

My first year on the island I did not take a very active part in the corridas. I was too busy with the cattle. I did ride in a few just to see what they were like and they were like no cow roundup. I have ridden in quite a few cow roundups and a corrida or wild sheep roundup makes a cow roundup look like a tea party.

Sheep are like deer in some respects. When they see a rider instead of heading down hill for the valley or flat land, where they can be driven in a bunch to the corrals, they head for the highest and roughest country.

The first step in starting the corridas was to recruit the vaqueros. This was done in Santa Barbara. It wasn't much of a job. They knew when the corridas would start in the spring and were waiting around. Of course each man needed a small advance to pay his bills. On receiving a few dollars they disappeared with a solemn promise to be at the boat early the next morning.

Most of them arrived at the boat in good time, some a little the worse for wear. There were always a few that failed to appear. On being asked "Where are so and so and so and so?" they never replied, "He is in jail." Instead they rolled their eyes, maybe sighed and replied, "Ah, pobrecito, está en dificultades."

That meant the boss had to go up to the county jail and talk Sheriff Jim Ross into turning them loose. This he generally did in return for the promise that they would not be back in town for two or three months. Sheriff Ross and his deputy sheriff, Johnny Longawa, were a couple of fine men. I came to know and respect them both over the years.

Finally they arrived at the island, a little bit late thanks to the "pobrecitos." Some were good sailors, some were seasick, and some just plain crudo (hung over) .

The balance of that day and the next would be spent getting settled in the bunkhouses, fixing up their saddles and riding gear, and trimming their horses' tails. A long-tailed bronc can be dangerous. If he picks up a branch or particularly a cactus leaf he may go to bucking and not stop until he gets rid of it and often his rider too.

The following day it would be clear out trails or varedas that had become overgrown or washed out and repair the punta mangas or wing fences leading into the corrals. The punta mangas were built of brush piled in a windrow. They might be from a few hundred feet to half a mile long. They had to be repaired before each day's corrida because, with cattle walking over them and using them for scratchers and wild hogs pushing their way right through them, they didn't last long.

The next morning horses were saddled before daylight and at dawn or a little before the vaqueros were off for the first corrida. Most of the men had ridden in many corridas on the island and knew every trail and what they were supposed to do. To any new men the mayordomo explained on the way out what was wanted and how to go about it. As we rode along he stationed men, usually experienced old hands, at various locations called puestos. These were spots where from past experience he knew the sheep were likely to break through into another valley or range of hills. If they succeeded the corrida for that day would be over.

The rest of the men and the mayordomo continued on, usually down almost to the ocean or as close as possible. At a signal they started up the ridges and canyons shouting and cracking their chiriones or bull whips to get the sheep started.

A chirrioñ is the most vicious bull whip I have ever seen. It is a tapered lash six feet long made of four strands from the heaviest part of a sun-dried cow hide. It is fastened to an 18-inch willow handle or stock and has a rawhide pajuelo or popper on the end. When you learn to use one you can make a pop like a pistol shot or raise a welt on a cow with it. I never saw one anywhere except on the island. They traced back to the mission days but had long since fallen into disuse on the mainland. A chirrioñ was standard equipment for an island rider.

The sheep, true to their instinct, started for the high country with the riders following behind, cutting down through canyons and along hillsides to stir up any that lagged and the next minute riding hard for some spot on a hogback or cuchillo where it looked as though the sheep were going to try to break through into some other canyon not included in that day's run.

This was where the men on the puestos had to keep their eyes open and anticipate where the sheep were going to try to break through, waving their hats, yelling and popping their whips or riding hard to get to some small saddle in the ridge before the sheep got there. If a few broke through it was very hard and sometimes impossible to turn the rest of them.

Finally the sheep topped the ridge and headed down hill only because no other direction was open to them. There might be five hundred or a thousand in the drive and it meant ride hard to keep up with them. Sheep can go fast downhill in rough country.

At last, if we were lucky, they were between the punta mangas. They were tired now and probably bewildered so they moved more slowly. A couple of men rode along the outside of the wings to prevent breakthroughs. The rest closed in behind as quickly as possible. Now it was a case of ride slowly and keep them moving in the right direction without crowding them. That could cause a breakback. Sometimes they would break back anyway and we would lose a whole day's drive. This usually happened right at the gate to the corral. Some old ewe would let out a bleat and start and the rest would follow her. They would go round us, under us, and everything but over us. For tired sheep they sure recovered their energy fast and even if they slowed to a walk when they reached the steeper slopes there was no heading them back that day.

Once in the corrals and the gates closed one would think our troubles were over but we still had the cholas to watch. A chola is a throwback to the old Mexican sheep as bald as a Chihuahua dog except for a little tuft of wool on the back and a little around the face. They were usually longer-legged and less blocky than the others and I have seen one of them run across the corral and clear a five or even a six foot fence as easily as a deer. When one of them did this the other sheep tried to follow and fell back in a pile. If we didn't get there quickly and break it up we had a bunch of trampled and injured sheep and sometimes some dead ones. Sometimes a few ran right up the pile like a ramp and made it over the fence. Any dead ones were sold to any vaquero that wanted them for fifty cents each on condition that he deliver the pelt to the ranch. They made jerky of the meat and I guess this was the winter meat supply for a lot of their families.

The day's corrida being safely corraled at Portezuela, it was time for lunch and a welcome rest for both men and horses before the drive to the main ranch and the shearing sheds started. The horses were watered at the stream, unsaddled to roll and graze, and the men sat around and discussed the day's work while lunch was prepared. This consisted of barbecued lamb, bread, and onions, washed down with a pint of piquette, wine cut fifty percent with water.

After about a two-hour rest the final run would start. The sheep were turned out of the corral and started down a steep canyon. Two men on good sure-footed horses started down the steep ridges on either side. Their job was to hit the valley floor with the leading sheep or a little ahead of them and keep them running straight on down the wide flat stream bed instead of turning up side canyons. The other riders followed to keep the herd moving and prevent them from cutting off across the ridges and returning to the hills.

On my first corrida I was selected as one of the lead riders, probably to try out the new cattle boss and see what kind of a rough country rider he was. The other man was Francisco Dominguez, a short, thick-set middle-aged man more Indian than Spanish. He was easy-going but a top notch vaquero and rider, also an artist with a reata. I knew that I was being tried out and Francisco could not let a new man beat him. That ride downhill over brush, rocks, and cactus developed not into a race with the sheep but one between Francisco and myself. We hit the flat stream bed just about neck and neck. Maybe we were spurred on a little by the fact that some movie company had obtained permission to film this part of the run and their cameras were set up at one side to catch us as we ran down the hill.

Along the sides of the valley at intervals were posted about everyone else on the island that could be spared from his job. These were vineyard workers, hay hands, and even the bull cook. They had been brought out in a wagon, some armed with sacks to wave and some with tin cans to beat—anything to keep the band in the middle of the arroyo and out of the canyons and brush.

For a short distance the sheep put on a burst of speed but soon tired and settled to a walk. A few even gave up and lay down, refusing to move. Most of these were what were called lana largas or long wools. The lana largas were long-wooled sheep that had never before been caught in a corrida and had as high as a six or seven-year growth of wool. Some of them sheared as high as thirty pounds. Of course with all that wool they gave out quickly. These were picked up and put in the wagon and hauled to the corrals.

The sheep or borregos, as they were called, being safely in the corrals at the Main Ranch the vaqueros on the following day became sheep shearers. The old California vaquero did not have the prejudice against sheep that cowboys in other parts of the country had. There were reasons for this that I will not at this time try to explain.

The sheep were herded into small pens in the shearing shed or trasquila. All of the shearing was done in the old way with blades. A husky young man could shear up to seventy or eighty sheep a day, some of the older men only forty or fifty. It was hard work and took a lot of practice to take the fleece off in one piece like a jacket, then a few odds and ends from the face and legs, roll it up and deliver it to the long table, where a couple of boys tied it with twine and tossed it in one of several bins according to grade.

From the bins the fleeces were tossed into large wool sacks suspended from a frame. Inside the sack was el sacador, a man who placed the fleeces and packed them tightly so that the sack when full weighed about four hundred pounds and made a tight, solid package. The sack was about seven feet long and once in it el sacador could not very well get out without help until the sack was nearly full, when he climbed out over the top.

A favorite sport was to tie a rope around the sack just above the sacker's head and leave him in the sack, preferably at lunch time. It was bad enough working inside a sack partly full of greasy wool on a hot day but to be tied in one called for a choice collection of Spanish oaths from el sacador while everybody else went into gales of laughter. The joke usually ended by the sacker pulling out his knife and ripping the sack open so that he could get out.

This particular sport was frowned on and forbidden but it always happened once or twice during the corridas when the boss was busy somewhere else. It did no good to ask who did it as the answer was always the same, "I was busy shearing, my back was turned, and I did not see anything, señor." Woolsacks cost $1.50 each, which was why we tried to keep the men from tying up the sacker but sometimes I think maybe the four or five dollar a year cost was well worth while to keep the men laughing on an otherwise tough, dirty job.

The Spanish loved a joke and once a joke tickled their sense of humor they never seemed to tire of it. It would be repeated over and over and always draw a big laugh. There was one shearer named Mazzini. He was a middle-aged man with a full beard slightly grey. One of the men had just finished shearing a particularly tough old toro coludo and as he straightened up and turned the buck loose he cried "Suelto Mazzini," I turn Mazzini loose. Everybody roared and for two weeks no shearer ever turned a buck loose but what he cried "Suelto Mazzini." It always brought a big laugh.

Back of the tying table, sitting in a sort of pulpit arrangement, was el fichero. When a shearer delivered a fleece to the table el fichero gave him a little brass counter called a ficha, two for each buck shorn. These were what they were paid on, so much for each ficha.

On the shearing floor was a boy called el aceitero, the oiler. He had a small pail filled with a mixture of pine tar and turpentine and a small brush. When a shearer would cut a sheep with his shears he would call out, "Aceite" (oil) and the aceitero would run over and paint the cut.

In adjoining corrals were the capador and his assistants, also the dockers who cut the lambs tails. El capador tossed the huevos into a large dishpan and at night the entire ranch had a big meal of mountain oysters fried in batter.

During the corridas fat lambs, wethers, and sometimes some fat ewes were parted out. These were put aboard the schooner and shipped to Santa Barbara.

This was just one corrida. There were many more to be run which I will not describe as it would be largely repetition. There was one, however, with an interesting side line, if you can call it that. It was the corrida that took place in the territory from the Sur Ranch to the Aguaje, a long stretch of country without any water except at the Sur and the Aguaje, where there were good running streams.

The sheep that lived in the central portion of this waterless stretch, unbelievable as it may seem, never tasted water from birth to old age except what they received from dew or rain or eating a form of ice plant called Siempre Viva. I have chewed Siempre Viva many times when thirsty and it is a good substitute for a drink of water. These sheep lived in a country composed of lime rock and were easy to recognize by the large amount of powdered limestone in their fleeces. They would spend three and four days in the corrals and never go near the water troughs. A few might learn to drink from the example of the other sheep but most of them just went thirsty and of course lost weight and suffered.

All of the sheep had to be held in the corrals until the last one was sheared. This was done so that each ewe could find her own lamb. Then the gates were opened and away they went. In a few days most had returned to their own range. A few hung around the ranch for a while but eventually all scattered to the part of the island that they considered home.

People have asked me why we didn't use sheep dogs to gather the sheep. The answer is that it was tried once.

A group of several Basques came from Winnemucca, Nevada, once and arranged to buy several thousand sheep. When they arrived on the island the superintendent asked them if they wanted him to go to Santa Barbara and get the vaqueros to come and round up the sheep. The Basques snorted and replied that with their dogs they could corral every sheep on the island in a week.

So they started their corrida in the area from Pelican Bay to Fry's Harbor, starting on the Orizaba Flats. The island sheep had never been worked with dogs and some of those old wild bucks took it as an affront to their dignity. When the dogs tried to head them off they promptly butted the dogs into the cactus and rock and mauled them generally. The Basques and their dogs arrived at the ranch that night tired, lame, and full of cactus spines but without a single sheep.

They were not to be beaten that easily, however. The next day they left for Santa Barbara and bought up all the cheap muslin they could find. They were going to build muslin wing fences such as were used in Nevada to trap wild horses.

After several days of constructing the wing fences they tried again. The sheep decided to try the fences out and hit them going full speed. Off they went with an occasional old toro coludo trailing yards of muslin from his horns and looking like Valentino in *The Sheik*. For several years there were long strips of rotting muslin scattered from the Orizaba Flats to Cueva Valdez. They gave up then and said, "Send for the vaqueros."

The sheep were rounded up, loaded on the boat, and put in railroad cars in Santa Barbara. They were then shipped to Nevada.

The story that came back and for which I cannot vouch was that when unloaded and let out of the corrals to be driven to the ranch they scattered to the four winds and a lot of them never were caught unless it was by the coyotes. Anyway the Basques never came back for more sheep.

The corridas, together with the shearing, usually lasted from some time in March until the weather got too hot to move the sheep, some time in May. If we gathered ten thousand out of an estimated twenty to twenty-five thousand sheep we thought we had done well.

By that time both men and horses were pretty well used up. The men were tired and many of the horses were matados, sorebacked and thin. A few of the best men were held over for the roundup of cattle and the rest cashed in their fichas and were paid off. Then with their belongings and sacks of jerky they boarded the *Santa Cruz* and returned to Santa Barbara.

RUSTLERS

$\mathcal{S}$oon after I landed on the island Mr. Swain told me that rustling was one of their big problems. Probably from the time that cattle and sheep were first raised on Santa Cruz this had been a problem but a minor one. The small fishing boats that put out of Santa Barbara, Ventura, and San Pedro to fish the island waters had never hesitated to shoot a lamb or a fat calf if they wanted meat. Perhaps a few yachtsmen too knew the taste of island meat. This had however never been anything but a small time nuisance.

Times had changed. The large purse seiners carrying a crew of from ten to twelve men, mostly Yugoslavs, Neapolitans, and Sicilians, had arrived in large numbers to fish for tuna and albacore. They didn't do things in a small way. If they wanted meat they went ashore in groups of nine or ten men armed with high-powered rifles and killed from one to a half dozen beeves and maybe three or four sheep. They then quartered them, leaving the hide on, and took them aboard their boat to be skinned out and cut up at their leisure. They left us the head, feet, and entrails. They were most of them powerful men and shouldering a quarter of beef and carrying it to the skiff offered no problem.

Occasionally riders had come on them in the act and the response was always the same. The fishermen grabbed their rifles and started shooting. I don't think they ever tried to hit any of the men but they sent their bullets too close for comfort and the rider, being unarmed, got out of sight behind a hill as fast as he could and kept on going.

Mr. Swain had taken the matter up with the local sheriff; the island being part of Santa Barbara County, it was under his juris-diction. However he was helpless for a number of reasons which he explained to Mr. Swain and later to me. He did not have enough man power to spare anyone for permanent duty on the island and to use his own words as nearly as I can remember them, "I have no deputy that knows anything about riding or living out in the hills as he would have to. You would have to spend your time taking care of him to keep him from getting lost or falling off a horse. It would be all wrong to send a man like that single-handed against a band of armed lawbreakers." His point was well taken.

Mr. Swain then appealed to the attorney general of the state and of course was referred back to the local authorities. But the prize answer was the one he received from the U.S. attorney general. Mr. Swain suggested that since we were still technically at war with Austria it would be a good idea to disarm all of the citizens of that country before they put out in their boats. This would have probably stopped a lot of the rustling by Yugoslavs. The attorney general sent a very unctuous letter saying that he could not bring himself to believe that the Austrian fishermen were anything but law abiding citizens with the thinly veiled hint that Mr. Swain was having a pipe dream.

About that time the fishermen sent word that they would kill anyone who tried to stop them. Mr. Swain made no more attempts to stop rustling.

When I asked him, "Why not arm the men including myself and let us shoot back?" he replied, "No, someone might get shot. I wouldn't want that to happen no matter which side he was on."

My first experience with rustlers was nothing exciting but very maddening and perhaps frustrating because there was nothing anyone could do about it. It made me determined to put a crimp in their activities if I ever got a chance.

Mr. Swain was away for a few days on the mainland. A purse seiner put into Prisoners' Harbor saying that they wanted to buy about a thousand gallons or more of wine. It was still legal to sell it in large quantities. They said they were in a big hurry as they wanted to get the wine to San Pedro, transport it to their homes, and get back out to sea to take advantage of a big run of fish that was on.

I took men off of other work and we delivered the wine as quickly as we could. Two of the men who looked like nice middle-aged family men said that they would sure like to take a couple of lambs home with them as pets for the bambini. There were some sheep feeding in the flats at the harbor and I managed to catch a couple of lambs which I threw in as pets for the children. They paid for the wine and set sail.

They stopped at the Scorpion Ranch and walked up to the house inquiring for the foreman. Dapelo, the cook, a slight, little old country Italian in his late sixties, explained that he was alone and the foreman and his helper would not be back for an hour or two. Their attitude immediately changed.

They told him to get back in the kitchen and stay there or they would use him for fish bait. They then went to a pen where a couple of wild hogs the men had captured were being fattened for salami and killed the hogs. At the same time they gathered up a half dozen hens and a rooster that were Dapelo's pets and made off with their loot.

That night the foreman called me on the single wire telephone and he was fit to be tied. From the description he had wormed out of poor old Dapelo, who was thoroughly scared, it was the same boat, *The Moonlight*, that had bought the wine.

The next night I was fit to be tied. I had gone to the Scorpion early in the morning to get as much firsthand information as I could. After lunch I started home and as I had plenty of time I decided on impulse to go the long way around by Smugglers' Cove, the Aguaje, and across the Vareda Molay.

When I arrived at the Aguaje I found that either they or some other boat had been there probably the night before. They had killed two beeves and thrown the heads, feet, and entrails in the water troughs. Putting two and two together I figured they had been high on the wine they purchased and thought this would be a fine joke. Sober men would not have gone to the trouble to pick up all that mess and put it in the troughs.

There was nothing much we could do about it. Dapelo was too frightened to identify anyone in court. The attorneys would have crucified the old man. There was no way to prove it was the same boat that killed the beeves. So there it stood.

Shortly after this I became superintendent. I then went through the same steps outlined above with one exception. When the U.S. attorney general sent me a letter almost identical with the one he had sent Mr. Swain I turned it over and answered on the back of it. I told him that since he could not bring himself to believe that we were having difficulty with the fishermen I hoped he would be unable to bring himself to believe that the fishermen were having difficulty with us if any of them so reported, and that we intended to protect ourselves and the livestock as best we could. I never heard from him again.

I also had another talk with Sheriff Jim Ross. He was unable to give us any direct help. He did however give me some very good advice on our legal rights, etc.

After becoming superintendent and having made every effort, without success, to get help from the authorities I told the men that none of them were hired to fight off rustlers. That I was going to start carrying a gun and did not intend to be run off if I caught any of them stealing cattle or sheep. I told them that they could carry guns or not, just as they wanted.

A couple of the men said that they wanted nothing to do with carrying guns. This happened in the morning just as we were about to start out for the day. The rest of the men walked over to the bunk house and came out with their guns strapped on. I didn't even know that they had them. I guess they had just been itching for a chance to put the fishermen on the run and get even.

My second experience was equally as frustrating as the first one. In the course of my riding I had noticed that some of the canyons and valleys on the south side of the island, Coches Prietos, Alberts, Orquetta, Los Álamos, and Los Sauces, had an abundance of good feed. The sheep had not moved in in any large numbers. I was later to learn why. All of these canyons had plenty of water and between feed and water it looked like an ideal place to fatten about one hundred steers. So we moved one hundred head into Coches Prietos, knowing that they would scatter out into the other canyons.

As this part of the range was just over the hills back of the Main Ranch and could easily be covered in a half day's riding, I took it on myself to watch this particular bunch. Usually I rode alone but sometimes I took another rider with me.

The cattle settled down and seemed to be satisfied and doing well, so I stopped riding over there every day and went only about twice a week. One day when I went over to Coches Prietos I saw a few cattle high up on the hills but none down in the flats where they usually stayed. When I rode down to investigate I found the heads and feet of about a dozen head. The same was true in some of the other canyons, heads and feet to show where they had been shot and butchered. The rest of the cattle had scattered, some to the high hills, some to the brushy country in Laguna and gone wild, and some had wandered back to their home ranges. The reason there were few sheep and lots of feed in these canyons was that the fishermen had chased them out by continual hunting.

This was good cattle country. The ideal arrangement would have been to put cattle there during the winter and spring when there were few if any purse seiners in those waters and the southeast storms made landing hazardous and at times impossible. Since we were short of feed and needed all the grass we had I decided to try a bunch of thin cows. They would be less of a temptation and I made up my mind to ride and guard them everyday. I was mad.

We put a bunch of cows in Coches Prietos and I rode every day early and late and also came from different directions. The cows settled down and were doing well just as the steers had done. I rode religiously for a couple of months and nothing happened. I was beginning to think I was wasting my time because riders would bring in reports of one or more animals being killed in widely separated places such as El Pozo, Punta Negra, Potrero Norte, or Smugglers'. I thought I might have more luck somewhere else and then it happened.

I had come along the ridge from the Sur Ranch and was about to turn down the long ridge separating Albert's Anchorage from Coches Prietos when I saw a purse seiner anchored in Coches Prietos harbor and a skiff with one man in it on the beach. There were a bunch of cows lying down in the flat back of a willow thicket that separated them from the beach. Some of the cows were moving about grazing. I started down the back side of the ridge looking over the top every little distance. Soon a group of about eight or nine fishermen armed with rifles came out of the willows and started stalking the cows. I was a couple of hundred yards away from them and I yelled at them.

Immediately some of their rifles came up and the bullets began to whine past me and toss little spurts of dust on the hillside below me. I could imagine that I could hear them laugh and say "Watch that cowboy head for the flat country."

Instead I dropped back of the hill and tied my horse to a tree and took my own rifle out of the scabbard. When the cattle heard the first shots they had taken off up the canyon through the brush. When I looked over the hill the fishermen were standing in a group probably discussing what to do next. I would have liked to have heard their comments and seen the look on their faces when they heard the crack of a rifle and the dust spurted up a little to one side of them. That was followed by one right over their heads. This one I had notched so it would whine plenty. They broke all records getting back into the willows.

I think they were really scared because they made no attempt to reach the skiff. They followed the willows and then up a small side canyon making a dash over a small hill that formed the western side of the cove. Once over the hill they had just as good cover as I had. In the excitement the man who had stayed with the skiff had rowed around back of the same hill.

The fishermen got in the skiff and started for their boat which was anchored a couple of hundred feet from shore in the bay. Just out of orneriness I sent a couple of shots right in front of them. They put back of the hill in a hurry. Now they were mad.

At least some of them climbed the hill and started shooting back in earnest. They didn't know exactly where I was so most of their shots were pretty wild. If they started getting close I dropped back of the hill and moved to a new position and sent a couple of shots in their direction.

How long this would have continued I do not know, but a heavy fog settled in so thick that I could not see their boat or the hill they were behind. I had no intention of staying long enough to let them outflank me under cover of the fog but I did stay long enough to hear them board their boat, start the engine, and pull out of the harbor.

All kinds of rumors about the fight came back via the grapevine, but my opinion is that both sides burned a lot of powder and nothing more. Cattle rustling did not stop with that one fight but it became less popular as did also the sport of making cowboys run for cover.

Later in this same canyon, Coches Prietos, Ramón Romo and I encountered a group of rustlers one afternoon. We had just topped the ridge back of the Main Ranch when we heard shots in the hills southeast of us near the harbor. At the same time we saw a purse seiner anchored in the harbor and a skiff on the beach. We decided to slip down the cuchillo and surprise them as they were carrying the meat to the skiff. We were too late. The lookout on the boat had spotted us and sounded several short blasts on the whistle to warn his shipmates.

We made it down to the willow thicket in time to see eight or nine men coming down the small side canyon. None of them were armed. I told Ramón to stay in the thicket and I would go out and talk to them. I walked up the canyon a short distance to meet them.

I asked them what they were shooting at and where were their guns. They replied that they had no guns and had heard no shots and were just taking a walk to stretch their legs and enjoy the scenery.

I told them that I knew they were lying and to get on down to their skiff, get out and stay out. They sort of laughed and the leader said that if that was how I wanted it they would get out. Some of them started down the regular trail which was about ten

feet below where I was standing but three of them started to take
a trail that ran just a couple of feet above me. I motioned with my
rifle and told them to take the lower trail. They hesitated a second
or so, grinned sheepishly, and took the lower trail.

As I ordered them to take the lower trail I half turned around
and could see Ramón concealed in the bushes and with his rifle
trained on them. When I got back to where he was I remarked that
he had had those three pretty well covered. He shook his head and
said, "I didn't know whether you were going to let them take that
upper trail or not but I wasn't." Ramón was from Sonora, Mexico.
He had the features of an Irishman but his mother may have been
a Yaqui. Maybe that old Yaqui had spent his youth fighting Mexican soldiers. One or two fishermen added to his list would not
have spoiled his night's sleep. He was a picturesque old vaquero.

Ramón showed his nerve on at least one other occasion. Six
of us had left the Christy Ranch early in the morning. Our object
was to fan out by twos and ride from the Christy to Punta Negra
and from there to Hazzard's Canyon catching and cutting any bull
calves we encountered. We would eat the lunches we carried with
us at Hazzard's, where there was feed and water for our horses
and return the way we came, picking up any calves we had
missed. We were never really out of sight of each other all morning and joined forces a short distance from Hazzard's. About this
time we heard shots in the canyon and on looking over the edge
we saw a group of fishermen shooting sheep. There were several
dead sheep in sight. I yelled and fired a couple of shots well over
their heads from my revolver. They did not return my fire but
headed up the canyon into a heavy stand of brush, all but one
man. He headed straight up a steep grassy hillside. I never saw a
man go up a hill so fast in my life. He didn't even stop to take a
breath. Of course he was encouraged by several shots well to the
right or left or behind him.

When I looked around I missed Ramón and asked where he
was. Pete Olivari, who had stayed back and taken no part, told me
that Ramón had put his horse into a run down the ridge to try to
cut the fishermen off at the beach. One old Indian against a group
of armed men took nerve.

I decided this was a chance in a life time. I knew the fishermen were holed up in the brush and could not get back to their boat. I had no intention of trying to arrest them and march them on foot all the way to the ranch, but I thought if I could get close enough to positively identify them I would have a case where I could get a warrant and a conviction. I announced that I was going into the brush after them.

Tom Ward, a young man who was riding for the company said, "You are not going in there alone, Mac, I am going with you." We rode through the brush and searched for some time but found no trace of them other than one freshly-killed lamb. We decided that they had succeeded in slipping over the ridge and down the next canyon. I afterward heard that they were holed up under a ledge back of a thicket of cactus.

Some one in the group suggested that it would be a good chance to pot shot us off our horses. Big Jerry Shively was with them and vetoed any such idea right now. Big Jerry was an ex-Montana cowpuncher turned fisherman. He wouldn't rustle a cow and had no use for rustlers but it was no sin in his book to shoot a sheep. In fact he probably considered it a virtue.

The Yugoslav and Italian fishermen were a tough, lawless crowd generally speaking and they were about as tough a bunch physically as I ever met. In some ways you had to admire them. The local fishermen out of Santa Barbara hated them. They could foresee the end of the tuna and albacore with the purse seiners picking up forty to fifty tons at a time with one cast of their nets.

The small boats fished albacore with a barbless hook. Once they chummed the fish by throwing sardines overboard, the school went crazy and would grab unbaited hooks or any other small object. It was then easy to pick up a couple of tons of fish before the school came to its senses and dived.

There were numerous incidents where purse seiners came on small boats with a crazy school of albacore, threw their net around small boat and all, and then ordered the boat to push its way out over the net. The purse seiner then proceeded to haul in the entire school of albacore. Their nets had a draw string at the bottom so that no fish could escape.

They met their match at this on one occasion. A purse seiner threw its net around Big Jerry Shively and ordered him to get out.

Instead of doing as he was told Jerry ducked behind his engine and opened fire on the purse seiner with a high-powered rifle. The austriacos, as they were called, were glad to cut loose a net valued at many thousands of dollars and get going themselves.

Jerry, like one or two others, occasionally tipped me off when the big boats planned a raid on the cattle. Usually their tips were false alarms, being just a snatch of conversation or a rumor they had heard, but on one occasion at least they hit it square on the nose.

The raid was to be in the Aguaje on a moonlight night. I was waiting for them. They landed from their skiff and started walking up from the beach toward where a group of cattle were grazing in a flat. Before they got within shooting range of the cattle I let out a whoop and fired a couple of shots in the air. They started on the run for their skiff as though the devil himself was on their coattails. A couple of them stopped and fired a couple of shots wildly toward the hill where they thought I was and then ran again. That ended that raid, except for a couple of shots I fired in the air to let them know that I was still around.

A short while later Cuate Espinoza and I exchanged shots with a group of fishermen at Aguaje Escondido and I drove another bunch out of the Aguaje one afternoon. The Aguaje seemed to be one of their favorite places to kill cattle. As far as I know that ended the rustling of cattle until just about a week before I left the island to take a job in Chihuahua, Mexico. The word had gone out that I was leaving and they probably figured I wouldn't be bothering them so they came into the water canyon and killed two head one day.

About the time that we had started carrying our guns and shooting back at the rustlers word came to me that some of the fishermen had put a price on my head and I would be killed if we continued to fight them. I didn't put any stock in the story and figured they were just trying to scare me out of doing anything about rustling, as they had my predecessor.

There were three events that happened fairly close together that lent some truth to the story or they may have been just coincidence. I have never been really sure.

I was riding across a flat near Aguaje Escondido when I noticed a purse seiner coming from the east and cruising along slowly not far from shore. As they got opposite me two shots were fired from the boat. Both of them came close to me. I did not make any attempt to shoot back as they were out of revolver range. Anyway I was more concerned with getting myself and my horse into a small gully that would give us protection. I was able to watch the boat and it turned and put out to sea.

I think they were cruising along looking for cattle grazing conveniently close to the beach. When they saw me they knew that there would be no fresh beef that day and their shots were probably just fired in spite.

On another occasion Ramón Romo and I had gone to the top of the ridge back of the Main Ranch to bring in a bunch of five or six horses that were pasturing there. As we topped the ridge we saw a small local fishing boat in the harbor of Coches Prietos. Suddenly there were two shots fired almost together from just a few hundred feet down the hill from where we were standing.

We instinctively pulled our horses back of the ridge and then looked over the top from a different location. We saw two men running down the hill heading for the cover of the willows that lined the creek. They both had rifles. We were unarmed as we had only expected to ride to the top of the hill, pick up the horses, and return to the ranch.

The hill that the men ran down was very steep and covered with shale. Our horse could not make very good time down it and besides if the riflemen had decided to take a shot at us from the cover of the willows we would have been sitting ducks. We decided to take the long ridge down where we could make good time and keep out of sight most of the way. Being unarmed I don't know why we wanted to chase them. It was one of those things a person does on impulse I guess.

The fishermen reached the beach, got into their skiff, and made it out to the boat before we caught up with them. We rode out on the beach and I called to the boat several times and finally Charlie Hansen, a good natured Swede fisherman from Santa Barbara that I knew well, came out of the cabin. After some palaver he got in the skiff and came ashore.

His explanation was that they were just a couple of teen-age kids he had with him. They had gone ashore looking for wild hogs and finding none had decided to take a couple of shots at a rock on top of the ridge. We came over the ridge just as they fired. They realized they had come close to us and that we might start shooting back. With that they had panicked and ran. I believed that part because they made it to the beach in nothing flat and never poked their heads out of the cabin while we were there. If what Charlie said was true and it probably was, I am glad we left our guns behind that day.

The third episode happened late one afternoon. I was riding above Albert's Anchorage when I saw a small boat anchored in the cove. I decided to ride down there more to let them know that I was around than anything else.

One could not ride onto the beach at Albert's as there was a rock face about nine or ten feet high that a horse might have slid down to the beach, but he could never climb up it to get back. It was necessary to tie your horse or hobble him and walk down. I intended to tie my horse to a small scrub oak that grew on the right hand side of the creek bed. Just opposite the oak was a spit of land that jutted out into the creek bed. It was about four or five feet high, ten feet across and maybe fifteen or twenty feet long.

It was a creepy feeling as I neared the spit of land to see a rifle barrel pointing at me through a sagebush on top of the spit. It seemed to be following me as I moved down the creek bed. That part may have been imagination, but I know I was never out of line with it. I could not see the man behind the rifle. He was concealed by the bank and the sagebush.

I started reining my horse towards the oak tree but all the while spurring him in the off-flank to make him sidle over to the bank the while talking to him, "Get over there, Boy, so I can tie you up," etc. I hoped to get close enough to the land spit to fall off the far side of my horse and have the bank between me and the man back of the rifle. If I could do that we would be even as far as any advantage went and I would have a chance to figure out my next move.

Just as I was about to fall off the unseen gunman stood up and said, "Hello, Mac." It was Frank Nidever, who was reputed to be a crack shot.

I replied, "Hello, Frank. You had me pretty well covered for the last fifty feet. What was the idea?"

Of course he denied having pointed his gun at me. He had just laid it on the bank while he took a rock out of his boot. That was why he was crouched down behind the bank. His reason for having the rifle with him was that he was just going up the canyon to see if he could get a wild hog, etc. I never could quite figure it. He was probably out after a hog as he said in the first place. Then I loomed up right in front of him. Frank was a pretty decent sort, certainly not the type to ambush anyone. I think it was just a case of panicking for a few seconds until he had time to think. If he had been as scared as I was he would probably have shot me and thought about it later.

There were other incidents that happened while all of this was going on. Riders who I had traveling by twos had run onto rustlers in Laguna and Cueva Valdez and had run them off. These men thought it was great sport to turn the tables on the fishermen and make them run for a change while they sent bullets over their heads and around them.

Then there was "the wild man." The wild man was a big, good-looking, good-natured young Swede named Frank Hansen. He got his nickname because most of the time winter and summer he went around in just a pair of trunks. He had built a shack in Albert's Anchorage with the announced intention of obtaining squatter's rights. This shack burned down so he built a better one in Los Sauces near the beach.

On the excuse that we had cattle over there that had to be watched, I moved José Espinoza and Ramón Romo into the shack. They were a couple of tough old Indians and not even the wild man wanted to tackle the job of running them out, so he moved to Campo Johnson and prepared to put up another shack. He was persistent.

I rode over to his camp, picking up Ramón on the way. When we arrived I found a freshly-killed lamb hanging up and a half dozen sheep pelts with bullet holes in them drying in the sun. Hansen was out in his boat which I could see him making for shore a little way out.

I did not want to precipitate a fight if I could help it and I did not want him to say that I had sneaked into his camp when he was away because I was afraid of him. I took a shoulder of lamb with a bullet hole in it and a couple of hides and told Ramon to tie them behind his saddle and I would meet him later on the other side of the ridge, that I was going to wait and talk to the wild man. Ramon was reluctant to go but finally took off and I saw him cross the low ridge separating Campo Johnson and Laguna.

The wild man landed and when he arrived at his camp after the usual greetings I told him what I had done and also that I was going to take the evidence to Santa Barbara and ask for a warrant for his arrest. Then I waited for the explosion that I fully expected.

Instead he grinned and said "You are going to a lot of trouble, Mac. That won't get you anywhere. It's a long trip from here to the ranch. Why don't you have lunch with me before you go? I have some good lamb stew that I will heat up." It's hard to hate a guy like that.

He was right. I wasn't even able to get a warrant on the thin excuse that I could not prove that the meat or the hides came from Santa Cruz Island because we had no brands on them.

I did however, through our attorneys, get an eviction order, which I insisted be served by a regular peace officer. Johnny Longawa, the deputy sheriff, came over to the island with me to serve it. Of course there were fishermen at the wharf in Santa Barbara who saw the deputy sheriff leave on the *Santa Cruz*. Undoubtedly some one of them put out in his boat to warn the wildman. He in turn probably thought I had succeeded in getting a warrant for his arrest. The story that I heard later was that he loaded his boat with all his possessions and put to sea. He overloaded it and it sank under him half way to Santa Rosa Island. He made Santa Rosa in his skiff and from there was taken to San Pedro by some of his fishermen friends. Anyway his camp was vacated when the deputy sheriff and I arrived.

It was a long ride from the ranch to the wild man's camp, over twenty miles round trip over rough country. I felt sorry for the deputy sheriff. He never complained and took it like a good sport. We did liven the trip a little with a shot or two at wild hogs.

That night sitting in my living room Johnny made a remark that I have never forgotten. There was a picture of the girl I intended to marry on the mantel. We later married and are still married. Johnny asked me who the girl was and I told him that it was the girl I hoped to marry.

He looked at the picture and was silent for a few seconds and then said, "Well, you are a damn fool. If I knew anyone as good-looking as that girl I wouldn't be out here on this island chasing cattle and cattle thieves while some other guy stole her away from me." It was good advice and later I took it.

As to the wild man, we never saw him again. I heard that he went to San Pedro and took up his old trade as a carpenter. I was sorry he lost everything including his boat, but it removed a thorn from my side.

Of course all of these incidents caused a lot of talk among the fishermen and some of the residents of Santa Barbara also heard the gossip and as they passed from mouth to mouth they grew and became really wild west. Some of the stories said we had a fisherman for breakfast every morning or almost as bad as that.

To show what I mean I will tell one more experience. The telephone in my office rang one morning and one of the men from the schooner which was anchored in the harbor told me that a boatload of men had gone ashore and cut down one of the largest of the live oaks that fringed the beach. He had remonstrated with them and they had told him to get back on the schooner and stay there if he knew what was good for him. He had then gone to the caretaker's house and telephoned to me.

When I got to the harbor they had loaded some of the larger limbs in their skiff and taken them aboard their boat which was tied to the wharf. They wanted the oak logs to make knees for a boat. They were just in the act of pulling out as I rode my horse to the end of the wharf and dismounted. They had burlap sacking covering the name of the boat both on the bow and on the pilot house. This was to make positive identification of their boat difficult if not impossible. It was a trick they always used when they came ashore to steal cattle or sheep.

Their boat was already about five or six feet from the wharf so I made a jump and landed on the deck of the purse seiner. I did not jump aboard with my gun drawn as I later heard the story told. I may have had my hand on my gun to prevent it from being jolted out of the holster.

I asked the man who appeared to be the captain what he meant by coming ashore and cutting down one of the finest oaks at the harbor. He immediately answered "No spik English," so I tried him in Spanish and he said "No spik Spanish." So I drew on my very limited vocabulary in Italian and asked him the same question. He suddenly remembered how to talk English with "Aw, what the hell do you want?"

By this time we were well out away from the wharf but I made them put about and tie up. Then I made them unload the limbs. In addition I pulled the burlap off that was covering the name of the boat and told the captain I was going to get out a warrant for him.

The following day I went to Santa Barbara to swear out a warrant. After some searching I found an assistant district attorney playing pool in a State Street pool hall. He seemed to be highly annoyed at having his pool game interrupted, but kept on playing just the same while he pretended to listen to my story. Finally he stopped playing long enough to straighten up and give me the following answer, "No, I won't give you a warrant. You have a lot of oak trees over there and I don't care how many they cut. Besides I have heard about you. You are nothing but a hired gun man and if I can ever get the evidence I am going to hang you." So that ended that. The island company was not popular in Santa Barbara because the owners did most of the purchasing of supplies in San Francisco and shipped them from there.

COW ROUNDUP

The corridas being over it was now time to brand not only the calves but all the other cattle. The island company, having no adjacent neighbors, had never branded any of their stock. The hide and brand law which had recently been passed changed all that. It was now illegal to sell cattle unless they carried a registered brand.

The company had owned for many years a brand that was used on casks and barrels but it was not suitable for branding cattle, so a new one had to be devised. I suggested S+ which was adopted and registered and as far as I know was never changed.[1]

Mr. Swain, the superintendent, was unalterably opposed to the use of ropes in handling cattle. He told me that within a year he expected to put into force a rule that no rider would even be allowed to carry a rope on his saddle. He admitted that he had tried to learn to use a rope but had never been able to master the art. Perhaps that was why he was dead set against it.

He had during the preceding winter gone to considerable expense in building corrals and a branding chute at the Christy all equipped with a squeeze gate. His orders were that all cattle be driven to these corrals and branded in the chute. This meant some long drives, two days from the Scorpion Ranch plus the time spent in gathering.

So in the morning we started for the Christy arriving in time for the noon meal. In the afternoon we gathered enough cattle to keep us busy the next day. It was a mixed herd of cows, calves, bulls, steers, and heifers. They all ran together on the range.

In the morning Mr. Swain arrived early just as we were ready to start work. He wanted to see how his corrals and chute would work. We had the fire burning and the irons hot but everything went wrong. Those cattle had never been through a chute. A lot of them had never been in a corral. They were very uncooperative. If we managed to force two or three into the chute at least one and sometimes two wound up on their backs with their feet pointing at the sky. Work would stop while we dragged them out of the chute and started over. By noon we had branded perhaps a half dozen.

After lunch Mr. Swain came out and saddled his horse with the rest of us. Then he turned to me with a grin and said, "I have to leave for the ranch now. We have to get those cattle branded somehow so let your conscience be your guide," and rode off. We finished branding that bunch by noon the following day and started gathering again. As long as I was on the island if any cow ever went through that chute she wandered through on her own out of curiosity.

After branding all of the cattle that we could conveniently corral at the Christy we moved on to the Forney Flats. We had no corrals there so we gathered the cattle in small bunches and cut and branded the calves. With the number of men available it was impossible to hold a herd once you started roping and branding large animals. We were also short of horses. Thinking we were going to work the cattle in a chute, we had only brought one extra horse per man with us. We cut a few fat steers out for immediate sale and drove them back to the ranch to brand.

We let the large animals go as I knew we would have to bring them all to the ranch soon to cut out steers that were ready to sell, cull cows, boludos, or lumpy jaws and I wanted to separate the heifers that were too young to breed and put them on some part of the range by themselves. We could then brand them in the corrals.

So back we came to the Main Ranch to work the cattle from

Buena Vista to the Sur Ranch as well as get fresh horses. Our caballada was pretty well worn out and in need of a rest. On arrival at the ranch Mr. Swain's only comment was "Did you get the cattle branded?"

It was about this time that Mr. Caire approached me one morning and said he would like to talk to me. He explained that Mr. Swain was leaving for another job and offered to make me superintendent.

As it was I had a letter all written and waiting to put in the mail accepting a job with a large livestock company in Montana. After some discussion with Mr. Caire and agreeing on salary, etc., I accepted the job with the island company. Santa Cruz offered a challenge that I didn't want to miss. It was probably forty or more years behind the mainland in its methods of farming and livestock management. It was in fact a piece of California of the 1870s and '80s. Spanish and Italian were the accepted languages unless one considered the dialect used by the Italian vineyard and farm hands when talking to me. This was a mixture of Spanish and Italian with a little English thrown in. For want of a better name one could call it Santa Cruz Islandese.

I had no desire to spoil the romantic aspects of the island, but I saw no sense in feeding from twenty to twenty-five thousand sheep to shear about nine or ten thousand and get a forty to fifty percent lamb crop.

It made no better sense to run bulls with the cows the year round in the open range. This resulted in the loss of many heifers that were bred too young and in calves being dropped at the wrong time of year, when the cows did not have enough milk to properly raise them.

There was also the question of rustling. This I hoped to be able to stop. These were just a few of the problems that offered a challenge to an ambitious youngster. I have always been glad I stayed.

The roundup and branding was not half over and now I had that to complete as well as all the other problems of running a ranch of sixty-five thousand acres. There were cattle to sell, the grape harvest time was not too far off, and fifty thousand gallons of wine had to be hauled to the harbor and loaded on a vessel before the deadline date when the law would no longer allow us to sell it. We just beat the deadline. The grapes had to be picked and hauled to the harbor for transporting to the mainland. The law no longer allowed us to make wine. Prohibition was in full force.

I was busy but my mind was set on getting the cattle branded and separated out over the range in smaller bunches wherever the feed looked best. The result was that I was in the saddle many hours every day. Some days I rode as many as fifteen hours and on one occasion I was in the saddle for thirty-six hours except for short cat naps on the ground or stopping to change horses or to eat. I kept five or six good horses working most of the time.

Rounding up and branding at the Main Ranch was not hard and all went smoothly. Here I could work with the cattle and keep an eye on the other ranch activities. It was the same when we gathered cattle at Prisoners' Harbor.

The Scorpion Ranch was a tougher problem. Due to an old custom which had become a tradition on the island I felt that I had to be at the Main Ranch after supper in the evening.

The story went that many years before the island had a super-intendent who was a student of Shakespeare or maybe he just had insomnia. Anyway he sat up most of the night reading and never got up until near noon. So he started a custom of ringing a gong after supper and all the men gathered in front of the office. He then assigned each man his duties for the following day. This custom had been carried on religiously by every superintendent since that time. I had already learned that old island customs must not be broken lightly. They must be allowed to fall into disuse gradually and so it was with this one. I never discarded it but if I was going to be away I either gave them their orders a couple of days ahead or, later, when I had an assistant, had him do it. During that roundup I kept the trail hot between the Scorpion and the Main Ranch. As often as not I rode the fourteen miles before daylight in the morning.

After finishing the general roundup, branding and sorting out the cattle that were to be moved to different parts of the range, there were still some wild ones in the hills that we called the Colorados on the south side of the island. None of these cattle had ever been brought in. They were practically all steers that had wandered into the hills and gone wild. No attempt had ever been made to corral them and the ultimate fate of most if not all of the wild bunch was to become meat for the fishermen. Each year the fishermen would kill a few of them and each year a few more would go wild so it kept their number about constant, maybe a dozen or more. I decided to bring them in.

There were two ways to do this. The first was to drive a bunch of reasonably gentle cattle over there and leave them for a few days. A few of the wild ones joined up with the gentle cattle and we drove them all out together. The rest had to be roped and tied to cabrestos.

A cabresto is a tame steer or bull that has been raised around the ranch, fed, and taught to lead. When taken out into the hills and tied to a wild one and turned loose the cabresto has an object in life, to get back to the easy life at the ranch. The wild one bucks and jumps and wants to go anywhere just so that he gets away. The cabresto, generally a larger, stronger animal, just plods on towards the ranch and in a few hours shows up at the gate with the wild one in tow and very much tamed down. If they didn't show up in a reasonable time you took the back trail and found where they had gotten wrapped around a tree or bush, freed them, and let them continue on their way to the ranch.

It was the only way to bring them in. If you tried to drag and haze one of them out of the hills on a rope he would fight until he became overheated, lie down, and maybe die. Tie one to a cabresto and turn them loose and in a few hours they both arrived at the corral tied together. The wild one would be halfway broken to lead.

But I am getting ahead of my story. Catching the wild ones was quite a sporting adventure and looked forward to by even the oldest vaqueros. The wild cattle were like deer. They came out in the morning and evening to eat and visit the water holes. During the day they holed up in the brush.

We would arrive early in the morning, mounted on our best horses, at the spot where from their tracks we knew they were feeding. As soon as we got anywhere near them they headed for the brush. Then it was ride hard either to head them back into the open or catch them before they got into heavy brush. If they

reached the brush we followed as best we could. Sometimes they
would cross an open spot or at least a spot sufficiently clear that
with luck you could get a rope on them. Once in the really thick
brush they were gone for that day. It was a lucky day if we caught
two or three of them.

Roping wild cattle in brush country was a lot different from
roping in a corral or arena or even roping in open grass country.
To begin with, a rider was lucky if he had a chance to swing his
rope even three times around his head before he threw it. Maybe
that was why amongst the old-time vaqueros it was considered
very much the sign of an amateur to swing your rope more than a
couple of times, and to look at your saddle horn when you dallied
brought shouts of warning, "No mira la cabeza del fuste. Vas a
trozar los dedos" (Don't look at your saddle horn. You'll get your
fingers cut off). I have seen old cowboys shy a finger or two. To
have seen many of our modern cowboys who are considered top
ropers swing their loops fifteen or twenty times around their
heads before they throw and then have to look down and hunt for
their saddle horn would have brought whoops of derision from an
old-time Spanish vaquero.

Some of them had a trick which I learned and have found very
convenient. I still use it sometimes. It was to carry your loop all
wrapped up in small coils in your right hand. This prevents its
catching on brush, getting around your horse's legs, etc. When
you learn how to use it you throw your loop out wide open on the
first swing around your head and are ready to let it go on the
second or third.

After catching a wild one we tied him securely to a tree with
short heavy ropes that we had brought along for that purpose.
Then it was back to the ranch for our lone cabresto. Our one
cabresto that first year (we trained a couple more for the following year) was a beautiful registered Shorthorn bull named
Butterfly Prince. Butterfly was a character. As a calf he had been
handled and taught to lead. The island company purchased him
and turned him loose on the range with other bulls, but that didn't
suit his high-toned tastes. He took up residence at the Main Ranch
with the milk cows and any other cows in the vicinity as his
particular harem.

How he learned about it and also the trails back and forth I don't know, but he did learn that there were milk cows at both the Scorpion and the Christy ranches and every so often he would make a trip to each of the ranches, stay a few days and come back home. He took it easy, taking a couple of days to make the trip each way. If you met him on the trail it was useless to try to turn him back. He just quietly walked around you and continued on his journey. He was very determined and calm about it all.

On arriving back at the ranch he stood patiently with his head over the ranch yard gate waiting for it to be opened for him. If after what he considered a reasonable time no one opened the gate for him he just reared up on his hind legs and came down on top of the gate with all of his sixteen hundred pounds. Then he walked in through the wreckage. Needless to say anyone who saw him hurried to open the gate and let him in.

It was this homing instinct that got him his job as a cabresto. All we had to do was lead Butterfly out and tie the wild one to him and turn them loose. In a few hours Butterfly arrived at the ranch with the wild one in tow. The wild one of course wanted to go in any direction just to get loose. Butterfly wanted to get back to the ranch where he was fed and pampered. He was a bull with a purpose, sixteen hundred pounds of it. The wild one didn't have a chance.

A night's feed and rest and we took him out for another one. We couldn't leave the captives too long without feed and water so our steer catching had to be geared to fit the ability of Butterfly to bring them in.

One old steer that we brought in was about twelve years old. He was a solid red and all skin and bones. He had probably lost all his teeth and would never fatten up. I bought him for what he was worth and gave him to Cuate Espinoza for jerky on condition that he would take the hide off carefully and make me a reata. He made me a really fine reata which I still count as one of my prized possessions.

The making of a reata is a complicated and interesting process. However since the reata has fallen into disuse amongst all except a very few of us old timers I don't think the reata makers put the care and work into their product that the old timers did.

Most of the reatas made in the present era are for dudes to carry on their saddles in parades. The working cowboy has changed from the fifty- and sixty-foot rawhide reata to a thirty-foot grass or nylon rope. A good reata costs about a dollar and a half a foot so maybe one reason for the change is economic.

The making of a reata begins with the selection of the hide. It should be of a solid color. This makes the strands of equal strength throughout their entire length. The hide must be removed carefully so that there are no cuts in it. It is then pegged out to dry thoroughly. After the hide was dry and stiff Cuate started at the outer edge and with a razor-sharp knife began cutting a strand about three-quarters of an inch wide. He continued cutting around and around until he had cut the entire hide into one long strand. He then wet this one long strand and stretched it between two posts, tightening up on it every hour or so. This was to make all parts of the strand of equal strength.

After the stretching the strand had to be trimmed. We had knives and gauges in the saddle shop, but to use them would have been against tradition and maybe put a jinx on the reata. The time-honored method was to cut an L-shaped notch in a post, then stick his knife in the notch and slowly draw the pita or strand through to cut it to the proper width. A second and a third time through with the knife set at an angle beveled the edges of the strand. Crude as it sounds the finished job was as good as could be done with an expensive set of tools.

Then came the braiding. This was where the real art of reata making came in. A reata that is braided too tight is easily broken and also very hard to break in. One that is too loosely braided becomes sloppy in warm weather, so each plait has to have just the right tension put on it. Most reatas are of four strands although I have one of six strands. For braiding, the strands are rolled into a sort of a flat ball called a tamal so that the strands feed out of the center. The strands are kept not wet but damp for braiding.

After the reata is braided it is again allowed to dry out thoroughly, or almost. Then a hole is bored in a post just the size that the finished reata is supposed to be. A couple of feet of the reata are poked and worked through the hole and then the entire length is pulled back and forth through the hole several times. This sets all of the plaits evenly. Next comes the intricate job of attaching the honda or loop in the end of the reata. The honda is a beautiful job in itself, being all made of a single piece of rawhide rolled and then braided around the outside.

After all of this the reata is tied loosely between two posts or trees. It is then rubbed with a liberal supply of unsalted beef kidney fat (unto sin sal). After this a round stick about an inch and a half in diameter is given one turn around the rope so that it will run easily and this is worked up and down the length of the reata until the fat is thoroughly worked into it. Now the reata is ready for use and after you have roped about forty or fifty husky year-lings with it you will have the best rope that was ever invented if you know how to use a reata.

There was more to the roundup than just cutting and branding. Fat steers had to be cut out and driven to the harbor to be sold and loaded on the boat—also some cull cows and boludos. Young heifers had to be driven to other parts of the island away from the bulls. All of this called for riding every day by a half-dozen men. Cattle when put on a new range tend to wander back to the range they are familiar with and have to be held by riders for awhile until they settle down and accept the new location as home.

Finally the roundup was over. Shoes were taken off the horses that were to be turned out and their feet trimmed. Some of the vaqueros left for Santa Barbara as they did every year for a week or so of city life and a rest before settling down to another year's work. This gave me a chance to look and take stock of some of the other problems. I welcomed it. It was a chance to do some office work, inspect the vineyards, ride over to Pelican Bay, and visit with the tourists and some of the celebrities that Ira Eaton had staying there from time to time. But best of all was either going for a swim off the wharf at Prisoners' Harbor or packing a lunch and going out by myself for the day to look at the cattle, eating lunch under a tree, and taking a half hour's siesta while my horse grazed either hobbled or on the end of my reata.

Note: 1. The island brand was registered on April 17, 1918, before McElrath arrived on Santa Cruz. See Helen Caire, *Santa Cruz Island: A History and Recollections of an Old California Rancho* (Spokane, The Arthur H. Clark Company, 1993) 72.

SANTA BARBARA CHANNEL

*S*ome of the sights and experiences I had in the numerous times that I crossed the channel between Santa Barbara and the island may be of interest to my readers. Most of them are unrelated and occurred at wide intervals of time so the reader can expect a hodgepodge of events all crowded into one short chapter.

There were times when the channel was as smooth as a millpond and others when it was savagely stormy and rough. I always marveled at the way the sturdy *Santa Cruz* took some of those big waves, climbing up one side of the wave and sliding down the other only to rise and start climbing the next wave.

On one or two occasions I had come to Santa Barbara and was staying at my sister's home on Bath Street. At one or two o'clock in the morning the telephone would ring and it was a message from Captain Olivari saying that a southeaster was brewing and he was leaving for the island in half an hour, and he didn't mean thirty-five minutes. To stay in Santa Barbara during a southeaster meant to risk having the schooner pile up on the beach.

I would call a taxi, get dressed, and arrive at Stearns Wharf just in time to get aboard the boat. Captain Olivari never kept any night watch. By the lapping of the waves against the hull he could tell exactly what was happening weatherwise. He didn't sleep with one eye open but he did sleep with both ears wide open.

Then would begin the three hour or more run to Prisoners' Harbor. The captain would allow no one on deck except himself and he was lashed in position behind the wheel with a strong rope. I could look out through the cabin portholes or through the door and see what was going on. Some of those waves looked mountain high and each big one looked like it would surely bury us under an avalanche of sea water. The *Santa Cruz* rode them out one after the other, largely due, I think, to the skillful handling of the old captain.

We could tell when we were getting into the shelter of the island. The wind became less fierce and the waves died down noticeably. Once we entered Prisoners' Harbor, both the sea and the wind became relatively calm. We would then anchor and sleep until daylight before going ashore.

If we were shipping cattle or sheep we always got away from the island as early as possible. We did this to escape the afternoon winds. The first trip that I made with cattle I met Chino Bronco, a real character.

Chino was a sort of a freelance vaquero. He drove cattle from Stearns Wharf, with sometimes one helper and sometimes none, around the outskirts of Santa Barbara to Gehl's slaughter house, as well as doing odd jobs of buckarooing for local ranchers. The cattle that he drove from the wharf were cattle purchased on the island by John Troup, who was the buyer for Gehl. They did not truck cattle in those days.

Chino was a man probably in the sixties with a full beard. He was, like most of the Barbareños, a mixture of Spanish and Indian. He had a voice like a fog horn. He rode a large horse and carried a sixty-foot reata with which he was considered one of the best men in the country.

The cattle from the island were a fairly wild, spooky bunch. When they hit the mainland they apparently became bewildered by the strange sights and bunched together. They were generally easier to drive than so-called tame cattle.

Occasionally, though, one would break away from the bunch when they landed on the wharf and start on the run towards Santa

Barbara. John Troup, who was responsible for the cattle once they landed, was naturally afraid that a rampaging steer or cow would hurt someone. He would shout to Chino, "I'll give you a dollar if you stop him before he gets off the wharf."

Chino was a born showman. He would lope along behind the steer until he reached State Street or was entering the Potter Hotel grounds; then his reata would shoot out with a zing and you could hear Chino's chingaros, cabrones and other expletives all the way to the Arlington or almost. The animal he was after would be neatly caught around the horns. That old boy just didn't miss.

My first meeting with Chino was at the end of the wharf where we were unloading cattle. John Troup introduced us. In reply to my greeting Chino said, "You know my cousin?" naming a successful and socially prominent businessman of Santa Barbara.

On my replying in the affirmative he said, "We had the same grandfather. My mother was a Santa Cota Indian. I'm a bastard" —all of this in a voice one could hear half the length of the wharf.

Amongst the old time Californios illegitimacy carried no stigma. It was treated as a perfectly natural thing. I can recall several men who worked for me at various times making the perfectly straightforward and to them natural statement "My mother was so and so. She lived with so and so. They never got married. I'm a bastard." No shame, just a simple statement of fact.

Often when we crossed the channel the dolphins would play around the bow of the boat. They were playing and enjoying themselves just as much as I was enjoying watching them.

On one occasion a huge whale about fifty or sixty feet long dove right under the *Santa Cruz,* coming up and spouting on the other side. We were on our way to Santa Barbara and I had been watching several other whales spouting and blowing about a half mile to the stern of us. It was probably during one of their migrations.

Speaking of whales, I saw what was probably a fight between a whale and a school of swordfish. I was riding in the Potrero Norte several miles east of Prisoners' Harbor when I saw a large whale rise out of the water about half a mile or more offshore. I don't think he cleared the water but a good half or more of his body did. As he dove headfirst his tail cleared the water and he hit it with a slap that I could plainly hear. He did this a number of times. I don't know how many, but it was at least ten or twelve. A few days later a sixty-foot dead whale was washed up on the beach near Santa Barbara. Men who examined the carcass said it had been killed by swordfish. It was probably the whale that I saw and his leaps were an attempt to get away from his attackers.

One time I spent a night and the following day on Edgar Van Bergen's yacht. It was a wonderful experience. Mr. Van Bergen and his wife, in company with Jim Lanagan, the old Stanford football coach, and his wife, were cruising among the Channel Islands and anchored in Prisoners' Harbor.

We were working some cattle in the corrals and they came ashore to watch us. I had just roped a large cow when my horse lost his footing and went down. My right leg was caught under the horse and I was dragged a short distance with the horse on top of my leg before I managed to free myself. No bones were broken but I had a bruised and very sore leg. However I finished the day's work.

Mr. Van Bergen invited me to have dinner with them aboard the yacht and when Jim Lanagan promised me a good rubdown I wasn't slow in accepting. After riding to the ranch and getting a bath and change of clothes I started back to the harbor. I think the thought of that rubdown was the only thing that kept me from staying home. I was stiff and sore by that time.

After supper they talked me into staying the night on the yacht. It wasn't too hard to do. The thought of saddling up and riding all the way to the ranch as stiff and sore as I was did not appeal to me; moreover, Jim had promised me another rub in the morning. They were all wonderful people and grand company which in itself was reason enough to want to stay.

The following day, which was Sunday, we cruised east for about two or three miles and anchored about a quarter of a mile offshore opposite the seal rookeries. I have been told that this is the largest sea lion rookery on the Pacific Coast. It is a big one. We then got in the skiff and rowed in close to shore. The sea was like glass and the water so clear that one could see the individual rocks on the bottom in water that must have been thirty feet or more in depth.

On the beach were several hundred seals sunning them-selves, each old bull guarding his harem of about thirty cows. There were many pups, still too young to swim, with their heads up curiously watching us just like any other puppies. The cows kept up an incessant barking, trying to frighten us away. The bulls would occasionally let go a few deep-voiced barks, sort of bored with it all and only barking from a sense of duty.[1]

In the water around us were large numbers of seals. They would dive under us or around us, coming to the surface and barking. They were mostly cows or young seals but occasionally a big bull would dive under us and come up with his big deep bark. To see one of those big bulls maybe weighing a thousand pounds or more give his tail a flip and shoot through the water with the speed and grace of a mountain trout is an unforgettable sight. I had seen the rookery from the bluffs above it but it was just a lot of seals on the beach and in the water. This was the only time I ever saw it close up from a boat and then to be favored with clear water and a sea as smooth as a millpond was as much as one could ask for.

One experience while crossing from the island to the main-land will always live in my memory. It has given me many good chuckles and I think has entertained some of my listeners when I have told them about it.

I was on one of my infrequent trips to Santa Barbara. When I arrived at Prisoners' Harbor it was a beautiful morning and not a ripple on the ocean. There was not a breath of wind and I was sort of sorry I was going to be stuck in town for a couple of days during such wonderful weather.

We started out and I was surprised when Captain Olivari ordered the crew to raise all of the sails. He knew more about the channel than I could ever hope to learn so I just figured that the old sailor saw signs that told him we would get a good breeze somewhere out in the channel.

Sure enough a little way out we caught a breeze, not much of a breeze but enough to fill the sails and carry us along at a very slow rate of speed. He then gave one of the crew orders to shut off the engine. This surprised me still more because at the rate the sails were moving us we would not reach Santa Barbara till late afternoon. I was about to ask him the reason when he pointed off to the south. It was still miles away but I could see the whole Pacific Fleet coming north through the channel. They were evidently on maneuvers and were pouring on the coal or I guess it was oil.

How Captain Olivari knew they were coming, I don't know, but he timed it exactly right to meet them in mid-channel. The old man apparently had it all figured out. The law of the sea says that a steamer must give way to a boat under sail no matter how small and Olivari was taking full advantage of the technicality. As we sailed directly into their path he ran the American flag to the masthead and turned to me and his weatherbeaten old face broke into a grin from ear to ear.

It was some sight to see those big battle wagons maneuver around us at a safe distance without ever slowing up. Once past they formed ranks just as skillfully and went tearing along to the north as though nothing had happened, with the foam flying back in a spray from their bows. All of this because a little old sixty-foot schooner and her captain decided they were not going to get out of the way of the whole Pacific Fleet. We probably got roundly cussed for it.

Note:
1. Today there are no sea lion rookeries on Santa Cruz Island, although the animals do come ashore to rest.

STAMPEDES

With all of the stories that have been written about stampedes, whether the author ever saw one or not, I think it is time that some of us who have actually ridden through one or more should put our experiences down on paper. I have been in one large and a couple of small stampedes of cattle. I have also been in one stampede of horses which, although not nearly as large in point of numbers, was more exciting than all of the cow stampedes put together. In the following story I am going to try to convey what they were actually like, starting with the stampede of over one thousand head of cattle.

It was a crisp foggy morning on the Forney Flats. The fog was so thick that it was impossible to distinguish objects one hundred feet away. It would have been a great white silence except for the monotonous crash of the Pacific Ocean breakers against the 100 foot high cliffs along the northern coast of Santa Cruz Island. At times, when there was a strong northwest wind and the breakers were running high, one could feel the spray on his face a half a mile or more from the ocean. Twenty miles away to the north across the channel was Santa Barbara but as far as we were concerned there might as well have been no one within a hundred miles.

We huddled around a small fire waiting for the fog to lift so that we could start gathering the cattle for the long drive to the east end of the island. Our plans called for us to make Portezuela the first night and with good luck we would reach the Scorpion Ranch at the east end the second day. Here we planned to scatter the cattle out from the Scorpion to the Aguaje. As it was, we knew that the delay due to the fog would make it a three day drive.

The fog finally lifted and we started gathering. A couple of riders started west along the flats, picking up the cattle as they went. The rest of us worked the quebradas or breaks and canyons in the hills, driving the cattle out onto the flats, where they joined the main herd.

It was late in the afternoon when we arrived at the Christy and I decided we would stay there for the night. The herd was too large for the corrals, so we had to night herd them in the open. This we did in shifts of three men.

The night went by uneventfully and again in the morning we were tied down by fog. We could not start the drive because we had a lot of cattle to gather between the Christy and the Main Ranch, where we planned to spend the next night. As a result of our late start we arrived at the ranch just about dark and here our troubles began.

To get the cattle into the corrals it was necessary to move them through a thick grove of large eucalyptus trees. We tried to move them through as a herd, we tried to get them through in small bunches, and we even roped individuals and dragged them through in hopes that the others would follow. It was no use. They milled and bawled and refused to move. These cattle had been on the island for generations. They had never had any experience with bears, mountain lions, or even coyotes, but the instinct was still bred into them to be afraid of thick tree growths at night.

It meant another night of herding the cattle in the open. We did not expect any trouble. The cattle would not move down the valley because of the thick trees and brush. There was no danger that they would try to climb the steep hills on either side of the valley and all that was needed was a couple of men to keep them from taking the back trail.

A couple of the men held the cattle while the rest of us went in to the ranch and ate supper. After supper, Cuate Espinoza, a real old California vaquero, and I came out with fresh horses to take over until midnight. The two men who had been watching the cattle then went in to supper. The cattle were tired from a two-day drive and showed little desire to wander. We rode back and forth across the arroyo, which was about a quarter of a mile wide at this point. As we rode we talked to the cattle, hummed, or whistled softly. A few individuals started back the way they had come but these we herded back to the main bunch and soon they all settled down for the night, most of them lying down.

We ceased our riding back and forth and sat our horses in the middle of the arroyo talking in low tones while we waited for the hours to drag by when we would be relieved at midnight. Perhaps we were also thinking how good a bed would feel. The time dragged slowly until just before midnight and then it happened. Maybe the horses in the corral became startled and started to run as the relief riders came out to catch their mounts. The sound of running horses or cattle will carry a long way through the ground. A man lying on the ground can hear it at long distances and animals can probably hear it at much greater distances. Maybe a fox barked or a night bird called. Whatever it was, the entire herd was on its feet in a matter of seconds and charging up the canyon under full steam. Cuate and I were in the middle of the road.

According to popular ideas, we should have raced ahead of the herd, taking chances on going down and being trampled. I think I yelled, "Get out of here," but it wasn't necessary. We both put spurs to our horses, which wasn't necessary either. The horses seemed to sense the danger and were putting everything they had into it. It was a wild ride at night over rocks, sand bars, and gravel banks for a few hundred yards. I shall always have a great respect for Alazan, the horse I was riding. He seemed to know it was his skin as well as mine. As we rode we angled sharply to the right, heading for a small flat area of about two or three acres which was about four or five feet above the level of the creek bed. Here we knew we would be out of the main stream of the stampeding cattle.

We made the flat safely and then the work began. We rode shouting and yelling alongside the cattle, even occasionally firing a shot in an attempt to turn them and start the herd milling. We finally succeeded in turning the leaders after they had winded themselves with their first mad dash. By that time the other riders arrived to help us. At the ranch they had heard the pounding rush, the bellowing, and our shouts, and knew what it meant. They were all old-timers and had been through stampedes before. A couple of the older ones had been through stampedes in the old longhorn days.

The cattle on the island were not longhorns. They were a very good strain of shorthorn cattle. Normally this breed is very gentle and not given to spooking or stampeding. The island cattle, however, had been allowed to roam free with no fences, seldom seeing riders and not regularly rounded up and handled. Until the hide and brand law was put in effect, about a year or two before I went to the island, they were not even branded. The island being all owned and operated by a single outfit, this was not necessary. They were gathered from time to time in small groups to cut the calves, and a few head driven to the harbor to load on the boat for shipment to Santa Barbara. A lot of them were shot and hauled off by cattle rustlers and this did not tend to make the rest of the cattle tame and gentle. They were a pretty spooky lot of cows.

We worked the cattle back to the bed ground, where we held them until daylight, when they moved through the trees and into the corrals without any trouble. However there were a number missing. These had split off in small groups or as individuals and gotten past us in the dark. We spent most of the day gathering them. Some were as far as six or eight miles on the back trail. The following day we made the fourteen mile drive to the Scorpion Ranch with no more trouble than was to be expected on this drive. For several miles the trail followed the ridge that is the backbone of the island. Along this ridge it is always windy and the cattle try to get down into the shelter of the canyons, for which one could hardly blame them. Then came the Montagnon, a high volcanic ridge that cuts across the main east and west axis of the island like the arms of a cross. (This may be how the island got its name, Santa Cruz.) Getting over the Montagnon is a rough, slippery climb over volcanic rock and with a large herd it is necessary to push them along in small groups, which takes time and a lot of work.

Once over the Montagnon it was an easy downhill drive to the

Scorpion Ranch, where we held them overnight in the corrals. The next day we spread them out over the range and, leaving a couple of the older men to ride and keep an eye on them for a few days, the rest of us returned to the Main Ranch. What had started out to be a routine job of at most three days had developed into a five day job of hard work and not much sleep.[1]

HORSE STAMPEDE

Two of us were driving a large band of horses from the Main Ranch to the Christy. Some were to be turned out to pasture and some were to be used in the corridas or roundup of sheep. (I have written about the corridas in another chapter.)

For the first eight or nine miles everything went smoothly. The horses traveled at a Spanish trot, well strung out. They had made this trip many times before and knew where they were going. At the rate we were traveling we knew we would make the Christy Ranch well before lunch time and have plenty of time to return home in the afternoon.

I was riding a beautiful black mare named Lisa. She was the fastest horse on the island, spirited and as tough as rawhide. I had broken her and started her training; then I turned her over to a very good vaquero to use in his string. Through an unfortunate accident Lisa had developed an unreasoning terror of a saddle. If one approached her with a saddle, she would attempt to strike it or kick it or to break away and run. She was the same when you attempted to mount or dismount. She would strike and kick but she never had made any attempt to buck, even when I was breaking her. It was because of this, perhaps, that I was rather fond of Lisa and thought that with patience that I could gain her confidence and cure her of her fear of a saddle. The rider had turned her back with the remark, "She's an outlaw and will kill someone. I won't ride her again if it means my job." I put her back in my string and had been riding her for a couple of weeks or more.

It was still necessary to use her with a tapojo or blindfold. A tapojo is a soft piece of leather about four inches wide with loops on the ends so that it fits on the headstall of the bridle like a browband. When I saddled her, I would pull the tapojo down over her eyes so that she could not see the saddle. Once mounted and firmly in the saddle I would reach forward and raise the tapojo. When I wanted to dismount, I would reach forward and lower it. As long as she was blindfolded she would stand motionless.

As we started down the steep, narrow mountain road from Buena Vista the horses started to bunch up a little more and a mare in the herd started kicking at every horse that came near her and was holding the herd back and causing them to crowd each other. I moved over to the high cut bank on my right to pick up a rock or pebble to throw at her and make her move out. As I did so my toe caught against the bank and turned my foot so that my spur gave Lisa a sharp dig just back of the cinch. As she leaped forward, my spur raked her from the cinch to her flank. Lisa had never bucked with me before but now she made up for all the fun she had missed. She would buck a few jumps, then run and then start bucking again. She kept up running and bucking until we were well out ahead of the other horses, which by this time had broken into a running stampede all on a narrow mountain road.

The road was cut into a steep hillside and wound in and out of the draws and gullies. Where it made sharp turns in the gullies the outside was built up with stone work from a few feet to twenty or thirty feet of practically sheer drop to the rocks below. As we approached one of the gullies, where I knew there was a long drop, I noticed that the tapojo, due to her violent exertions, had dropped down over Lisa's left eye. This was on the side of the dropoff.

My thoughts at the time were, "Maybe you will make it around the turn and maybe you will buck off into thin air. Whatever you do you will do it alone." I unloaded fast. By good luck more than anything else I landed feet first but then lost my footing and fell across the road with my back to the oncoming horses. I did not have time to get up or even roll off the road before the first of them were sailing by me and some of them over me. All I could do was lie still covering my head with my arms as best I could and hoping that they didn't come bunched up so that they would fail to see me.

Horses are different from cattle. If there is a sack, a man or other foreign object in the road, horses will shy away from it or jump over it. Most cows will do the same, but there are always some in a herd that will land on it with both front feet. Maybe they work on the principle of getting in the first lick. As it was, if I had attempted to get up I would probably have been knocked down, kicked, or trampled, maybe all three. As my back was to the oncoming herd, I could not be sure when the last one had passed, so I lay there for a few seconds to be sure.

When I rose to my feet my companion, who had held back so as not to bunch the horses, exclaimed, "Gracias a Dios. Pensé que era muerto." (Thank God. I thought you were dead.) He was pale under his tan and I guess I was the same. Yes, I was scared.

I walked the last few miles to the ranch, where we corraled the herd and were in time for lunch. When the men at the ranch heard the story there was much shaking of heads and such remarks as "Patron, you should shoot that mare. She is an outlaw and will kill somebody."

As for Lisa, she ran right on past the ranch over a low range of hills into Cañada Los Sauces, then over another range into Los Pozos. We followed her tracks that afternoon. The trail then led into the rough Sierra Blanca. We gave up for the day and went back to the ranch. The following morning we found her within a half mile of where we had abandoned the trail the day before. Her jaquima rope, which was loose, had wound around a bush and stopped her. She was badly gaunted up from her long run and no food or water but otherwise alright as were my saddle, rope, and even my jacket, which was tied behind the saddle. We led her back to the ranch where she could get food, water, and rest before returning to the Main Ranch the following day.

Poor Lisa was an outlaw but a man-made outlaw. Through no brutality or intentional bad treatment but just a couple of unlucky breaks, she changed from a beautiful and gentle animal into a half-crazy outlaw. Less than a week after this episode, she came to an outlaw's end. She had never bucked before but now she bucked everytime I got on her. One morning she reared over backwards, hit her head on the ground, and broke her neck. Again luck was with me and I landed clear.

Note: 1. Some have taken exception to some of McElrath's recollections. Justinian Caire, in an undated letter on file at the Santa Cruz Island Foundation, Santa Barbara, California, questions McElrath's accounts of the stampede and encounters with the outlaw horses. Caire was the grandson of Justinian Caire, who had sole ownership of the island from 1880 until his death in 1897. The grandson was a cattleman on the island for a number years for the Caires and Stantons.

OUTLAW HORSES

A few horses are born outlaws but only a very few. Most outlaws are man-made. A horse may be made an outlaw in many ways but it is usually abuse, ignorance, or some unfortunate accident, and in some it is just a bad reputation.

We had several so-called outlaws on the island. The outstanding one was Saturno. He was a tall, rangy, good-looking bay. When I took over the job of bronc rider I was forbidden to even attempt to ride him. "That horse is a killer. He will throw you and then come for you with all four feet."

Saturno had been broken by a very good rider named Jockey Valenzuela. Jockey made the boast that no one but himself would ever ride Saturno and to this end he spurred him into a buck every morning. He also abused him until he made him head shy. It was a fight to put a bridle on him.

After the corridas were over Jockey had left for Santa Barbara and Cuate Espinoza added Saturno to his string. The first time Cuate tried to ride him he was thrown. He landed between the horse and the corral fence and rolled against Saturno's heels. This caused the horse to lash out. He missed Cuate but hit a redwood fence post hard enough to leave his footprint imbedded in it. From this grew his reputation. The print was pointed out to me with awe as proof that Saturno had deliberately tried to kill his rider after throwing him. Cuate scoffed at all of this and said he had been willing to get back on after being thrown, but the superintendent would not let him.

Saturno's next bid for fame was in the movies. A company was making pictures at Pelican Bay and the script called for the hero and heroine to make their escape from their pursuers by riding a horse off a seventy-five foot cliff above the ocean, dive clear of the horse, miss the submerged rocks, and swim to a ship that was conveniently anchored off shore. In those days it was easy to get movie-struck stuntmen to take that sort of chance for a few dollars.

Just west of Pelican there was an ideal spot, a high perpendicular cliff, submerged rocks with the waves breaking over them. Everything except a horse. Mr. Swain decided it would be a good way to get rid of Saturno and made a deal with the director.

Saturno had other ideas. First the movie cowboys got him mad by holding him by the ears while they bridled him and the two stuntmen got on his back. They then turned him towards the cliff and turned him loose while the cameras started grinding. Instead of dutifully jumping over the edge of the cliff he whirled around and in one or at most two bucks unloaded the stuntmen and took off on the dead run. Somehow he managed to rub the bridle off (the script had called for the stuntmen to ride him without a saddle), and was next seen contentedly grazing with a bunch of horses that had been turned out. It was at this time that Mr. Swain told Cuate to catch Saturno and shoot him.

Cuate had told me when we were riding together that he could have shot Saturno anytime but always reported that he had been unable to find him. "That is too good a horse to shoot. Any horse will kick at something that rolls against his feet when he is excited. You could ride him and he would make you a fine horse. Let me show you how to bridle him and after that you will have no trouble." And there it stood; I had been given orders not to attempt to ride him.

When I became superintendent the first thing some of the men asked me was when I was going to ride Saturno. I admit that after all I had heard I had no great hankering to ride him. But I knew I was on the spot so assuming an air of indifference I said, "Well, get him in this week and I'll ride him Sunday morning so everybody can see the show."

Good old Cuate in the meantime gave me some valuable tips. He asked me to let him bridle Saturno because he knew the horse and could get a bridle on him without too much fuss. He also suggested that I use a tapojo in mounting, because Saturno was a fast starter and would not let me get set in the saddle before he started bucking.

Sunday morning came and so did everybody on the island who could get there. We saddled Saturno and I mounted. Yes, I had a few butterflies in my stomach. I leaned forward and raised the tapojo. I could feel that big horse gather himself. It looked like a long way to the ground and the ground didn't look soft. Then he let go. I don't think I ever had a horse jump any higher. The thought flashed through my mind that if I ever went off it was going to be a long, hard drop but I also had time to get my feet forward and brace for the jolt that I was sure was coming when he hit.

To my surprise there was little or no jolt when he hit. It was like riding a horse with a high rolling lope. The bucks that followed were the same, high and spectacular but easy to ride. After six or eight jumps he quit and wouldn't buck even when I used my spurs. And so it was from then on. Any time he felt good he would make six or eight very showy bucks and then settle down to be a good true horse the rest of the day.

After that first ride I realized that he was mostly bad reputation. The old rascal had scared most of the riders off his back instead of actually throwing them. That first high jump loosened them up and they were glad to get out of the saddle about the second jump.

Saturno was not a fast horse. He had a good rein but nothing exceptional. But he was one of the best to carry you all day over the roughest country, come in at night all gaunted up, and the next morning be filled out and round and ready to give you your morning ride. The old boy and I got to be good friends. We got to be good enough friends that with a little coaxing I could walk up and catch him out on the range, take the saddle and bridle off the horse I was riding, and put it on Saturno and turn my horse loose.

After a few get-acquainted bucks Saturno and I would settle down to work together. That was a man-killing outlaw that had been sentenced to be shot. Saturno never was an outlaw. He was a good horse that had been taught that he was supposed to let go with a few bucks when anyone got on him.

Reputations die hard. Even after I had been riding Saturno for a long time some of the men insisted that he would kill anyone else who tried to ride him. Dour old Abelino Lugo, the stablebuck, went one step farther. When I would be saddling Saturno he would croak in his sepulchral voice, "That horse he just waiting for a chance. Some day he gonna keel you," and then turn away shaking his head.

Furia was an outlaw not from abuse, ignorance, or accident. She was just a lady with a mind of her own and a lot of pride and dignity. She was a real lady. She was gentle in that she liked to have her nose rubbed and her neck patted. The first time that I put a set of shoes on her—and as far as I know it was the first time she had ever been shod—I had no trouble with her at all. This was unusual, to say the least, with island horses.

Cuate Espinoza had broken her to be driven in the superintendent's Petaluma cart. After he thought she was thoroughly broken and safe Mr. Swain tried her out. Something spooked her or maybe she had her own ideas. Anyway she ran away and gave him a wild ride for a quarter of a mile or more before he stopped her. He would never drive her again.

The next day he had one of the men put her in as a wheeler on a four-horse wagon team. She started a run-away and smashed up the wagon. Then they tried her in a four-horse team pulling a harrow. She did the same thing, started a run-away and turned the harrow over, skinning some of the other horses up pretty well but not getting so much as a scratch herself. All of this happened before I came to the island and was told me by either Cuate or Mr. Swain. I had never seen Furia except at a distance out on the range.

Cuate in telling me about it and affirming what I had heard shook his head and said, "I don know qué pasó (what happened) with that yegua (mare). She was so nice and gentle when I drove her." I know. Cuate was quiet, easy, and gentle and loved horses and dogs and they knew it.

When I saw Furia out on the range she was a good-looking true black, the kind that does not turn brown in the sun. She was fat as a pig and looked like a small Percheron. In fact she was by a Percheron stallion out of a small Arizona mare named Sirena.

We needed work horses and I told a couple of the men to bring Furia and a couple of others that were running together in and we would put them to work. I planned to put a buck strap on Furia that would prevent her running away.

The next day I told a couple of the men to use the horses we had brought in and leave the ones they had been using in the corral for a few days' rest. This was all right until I told one of them to use Furia. Right away he had a good reason not to use Furia today but maybe he could use her tomorrow. So it went. Nobody wanted Furia. They knew her too well.

Sunday morning came and as usual I went down to the corrals to look the work stock over for any that might have collar galls, lameness, etc. While there I took a good look at Furia. She was not a work horse. Her fine limbs, neck and head were those of a saddle horse and a good one. Her only trouble was that she was as fat as a pig, which made her look like a work horse at a distance. I liked her looks and decided right there that I would make a top saddle horse out of her in spite of her being twelve years old and having a bad reputation. Such is the cocksureness of youth.

I called Cuate and told him to saddle up and ride herd for me; I was going to try Furia out. He answered "Sí, patrón, but I think that mare is going to give you a lot of trouble. She is already spoiled and never gonna be no good. Maybe you better turn her out with the brood mares."

He was partly right. She gave me a bad time. It took all the strength and know-how that I had to stay with her. In those days I had a lot of strength anyway. So it went every morning for ten days or more; it was a battle and sometimes another one after I had ridden her for a couple of hours.

In one of the mid-morning battles Furia won out. She threw me higher than a kite. That was my lucky day, however. Cuate and I were riding back to the ranch from Prisoners' Harbor. The road to the ranch had been cleared of rocks and boulders through the creek bed. It wound through an area of perhaps fifty acres that was nothing but rocks and boulders. When I went off I landed in a patch of pure sand perhaps not over ten feet wide in any direction. Anywhere else I would have landed amongst rocks.

Luck was still with me. When Cuate saw her start to buck he had shaken out a loop in his reata and just as I went off his rope settled around Furia's neck in as pretty a horse catch as one could ask to see. She never had a chance to run and go crazy. Maybe she thought that by some magic I had jerked her in a half circle and nearly thrown her off her feet. Cuate was a good man to have along in a tight spot.

Shortly after that Furia decided to quit bucking. It was as though she said, "O.K., you always treat me well so I'll go along." I got into several tight spots with her and she never showed any inclination to buck again.

Furia was high-headed and spirited with lots of speed and unlimited endurance. She had a wonderfully smooth Spanish trot. She was a completely trustworthy horse that a child would have been safe on. She, like Saturno, would let me catch her out on the range with one difference. No matter how long she had been running free she made no attempt to buck when I mounted her or even touched her with the spurs.

I do hope though at Judgment Day I will be forgiven some of the lies I told Mr. Caire about her. They were all told, however, to keep her out of poor hands.

The Caire family, when they visited the island in summer, always commandeered some of the best horses for their personal use. They were not experienced horsemen and the horses and their training suffered. Furia was a beautiful animal and I was sure Mr. Caire had his eye on her for someone of the family. About every so often he would ask me, "How is Furia coming along? Is she thoroughly gentle and trustworthy?"

I would answer with a straight face and a shake of my head, "I don't know, Mr. Caire. She is gentle as a kitten on flat ground or when she thinks you are watching her. Get on a rough trail and relax a little and the first thing you know her head is down and she is bucking like a wild horse. She gave me a bad time yesterday going down into the water canyon," or Cueva Valdez or some other location. No one ever asked to ride her.

Some of the men overheard my conversations with Mr. Caire and must have believed me because her reputation as an outlaw grew every time they repeated the story. When I left the island no one would ride her, according to what one of the men I met in Santa Barbara told me, so they bred her and turned her out with the brood mares. She was a grand horse but she had dignity and self-respect and you couldn't push her around. Maybe some will pooh-pooh that statement but I believe it. I have known more than one horse and many dogs that were easy to get along with as long as you realized that they had self-respect.

Lisa was a full sister to Furia and if anything a more beautiful and finer mare than Furia. She could show her heels to any animal on the island. She showed no inclination to buck when I broke her and was coming along fine. I had too many horses in my string so I turned her over to Ike Newton, a good hand, to finish her training.

Lisa was the same mare I spoke of in the chapter on stampedes. I am writing this just to show how one act of carelessness, forgetfulness, or maybe just an accident can start a fine gentle animal on the road to becoming an outlaw.

Ike liked her and was taking a lot of pains with her training. She was still a little spooky about saddling so he continued to use a blindfold or tapojo. He had gotten her to the point where he could unsaddle her without the blindfold by being easy and quiet with her.

Ike was left handed. He carried his rope on the left side of his saddle and tied his jáquima rope on the right side.

One evening as he was unsaddling her he forgot to untie his jáquima rope and as he lifted the saddle off of Lisa's back the pull on the rope caused Lisa to spin halfway around and knock the saddle out of his hands. Lisa went crazy. She tore round and round the ranch yard kicking at the saddle, which was dragging at her heels. She kept this up until roped and choked down and what was left of the saddle was untied from the rope.

It was a few days later that Ike gave her back to me, saying, "She's an outlaw and will kill somebody." He didn't say whether she had bucked with him or not, but I suspect that she had. Maybe she piled him. I rode her for some time but could never get her over her fear of a saddle although I tried every way that I knew. That one unfortunate accident had driven her loco. She never bucked with me until that first time as told in "Stampedes." There again was another accident when my toe caught on the bank causing my spur to give her a vicious rake. She was born to bad luck.

Maggie was that rare exception. She was a born outlaw. Maggie was a large fine-looking sorrel. She was broken by a man who worked at the Scorpion Ranch before I came to the island. According to what the men told me she was not a bucker. She would just rear up and fall over backwards anytime she got the least bit excited.

Maggie hadn't been ridden for several years and I thought maybe she had forgotten about falling backwards so I decided to try her out. I took the precaution of having another rider snub her down to his saddle horse and start her off at a run as soon as I got into the saddle. She tried to rear but being unable to do so let out a few bucks and settled down. I rode her tied down to another rider's horse for a few days and she showed no further inclination to buck or rear, so I started using her around the ranch, back and forth to the harbor and all the while taking it easy with her. I had no trouble with her at all.

I know now why it was that I had no trouble with her. Maggie was what is called a cinch-binder. Anytime you tighten the cinch the first thing in the morning they will get mad, some buck, some rear, and some rear right on all the way over. Others stand still and balk. I always have and still do ride with a loose cinch. The reason I can do this is that I learned to ride Indian style with just a rope around the horse's lower jaw and no saddle. The result is that I ride the horse and not the saddle. How to handle a cinch-binder is one of those things that you learn as you grow older.

I was sending Ramón Romo out to the Christy Ranch to ride and watch the cattle. He would have a lot of ground to cover but no hard riding to do. He would need an extra horse and as he had asked me several times to let him have Maggie I decided to do so. She was strong with a fast walk and an easy Spanish trot and I thought she would be just the horse for him to cover distances with.

From time to time when I would see Ramón I would ask him how he was getting along with Maggie. His reply was always the same, "She is a fine mare and we get along fine." This went along for some weeks.

One day Ramón came to the Main Ranch in company with the foreman. Ramón was riding Maggie. We were parting out some cattle from a bunch we had gathered and they came into the corral to help us. Suddenly Maggie reared and fell over backwards. Ramón landed clear of her. I afterward found out he had had a lot of practice.

As Ramón got to his feet he said "Dónde está mi palito?" I asked the foreman, "What does he mean by 'Where is my stick?'" Then the story came out. Whenever he laid Maggie off for a couple of days or whenever she got excited she tried to throw herself over backwards. Ramón had a stick like a billy club and would hit her between the ears and knock her down.

This is an old method of breaking a horse of the habit of rearing that I have heard of ever since I was a boy. I never tried it myself but I have seen others try it. I must confess that I never saw a horse that really had developed the habit broken of it by this or any other method. You can prevent them from rearing with a strong tie down that they can't break—but you only prevent them, you don't cure them.

I guess it was pride. Ramón had not wanted to admit that he was unable to cure Maggie so he always said she was doing fine. On the other hand, I did not want a rider out in the hills somewhere with a saddle horn driven through his chest or stomach so I told him to turn her loose in the corral and gave him another horse.

Later we bred Maggie and turned her out with the brood mares. In the course of time she had a beautiful little grey horse colt. I saw and admired him several times when out looking the mares over and then one day I missed him. After some hunting I found him just about dead from starvation. Maggie had deserted him. I drove the mares up to where he was to see if Maggie would claim him. She would have nothing to do with him. He was beyond help anyway and the only thing I could do was put him out of his misery with a bullet. I was angry and who wouldn't be? The more I thought about it the angrier I became. That mare wouldn't work and then she deserted her own colt and let it starve to death. I rode back to where Maggie was grazing and put her out of her misery too.

Maggie was a born outlaw in my opinion. Perhaps Ramón's hitting her between the ears to keep her from rearing may not have helped her mental equilibrium. I am sure it did not do her any good, but she was bad medicine before he ever got her and he had to protect himself.

Lisa was a gentle spirited horse that was driven crazy by a couple of unfortunate accidents, both the fault of her riders. I was one of them.

Furia never was an outlaw. She was a lady with dignity and self-respect. Perhaps she felt it was beneath her to pull a wagon or a harrow with a rough, heavy-handed teamster holding the lines. Once we worked it out between us I never had a truer, better saddle horse.

Saturno was just an old rascal. Maybe he enjoyed his reputation. I think he actually did enjoy trying his rider out in the morning. It was a challenge to both of us and added a little spice to the day. I enjoyed riding him and after our morning workout I knew that I had a strong reliable horse under me for the rest of the day.

graham ©

EL VAQUERO VIEJO

Joe Espinoza or Old Joe or El Viejo, as he was variously called, had worked for the Santa Cruz Island Company for many years, but before I came to the island he had had a run-in with the superintendent and had been let go. José was an old Spanish vaquero past 80 years old; he did not know his exact age, but he had been born a subject of Mexico in Santa Barbara and had seen Fremont raise the first American flag in that town, had roped grizzly bears for the bull and bear fights, knew Joaquín Murieta, Three Fingered Jack, and Vásquez, and had driven cattle from Los Angeles to San Francisco many times.

José was camped at Campo Chino, about two or three miles from Prisoners' Harbor, fishing crawfish for a living. In getting into his skiff he dragged his .30-.30 in by the muzzle. The bullet took the first joint off of two of his fingers, glanced around a rib, and lodged under the skin on his back.

He wrapped the stumps of his fingers in a bandanna and rowed all the way to Prisoners' Harbor. His reason was that he couldn't reach the bullet to cut it out and wanted someone to do it for him. He was quite disgusted and considered us all a bunch of sissies when we refused to do it for him and the superintendent put him on the boat and sent him to Santa Barbara for medical aid.

He never told me why he was getting into his skiff with a .30–.30. Maybe we had one more calf at branding time. I never worried too much about it. It was costumbre.

The next time I met him was when I had become superintendent and we were dehorning a large number of cows at the Scorpion Ranch at the east end of the island. Dehorning cattle in those days was a rough, brutal job. We roped them and stretched them out and sawed the horns off.

José had returned to the island and was camped at Potato Harbor. After finishing work the first day, we were eating supper when José showed up. He said he had come to visit with some of his old friends and his brother Cuate. The old coyote didn't fool me any. I knew he had come to hit me up for his old job.

We were shorthanded and I liked the old boy's looks, he was a fine specimen for an old man, and I put him on, for a few days as I told him. Those days stretched into several years or as long as I was on the island.

José was about medium size, slender and wiry, was fast and definite in all his movements. He had good aquiline features, showing his Spanish blood, but his Indian blood showed in his black eyes and many of his personal characteristics. He had probably been very good looking as a young man.

When we went to work the next day José proved to be all that was said of him. He was an artist with a reata, a fine rider, and knew cattle. Many of our horses were cold-backed or reparoso as we called them, meaning that when you got on them in the morning you were due for from one to a dozen stiff-legged bucks. In spite of his age this never bothered José. He would ride any horse that came along. I never gave him any bad horses but sometimes out on the range some rider would have a horse that he was afraid of and then I would see Joe coming in riding the bronc and the other rider on the gentle horse. Joe's answer would be, "El bruto iba a matar al pobrecito" (The brute was going to kill the poor fellow).

As time went on I took to taking Joe with me when I had a long trip to make. I would get him to telling me stories of the early days, which he loved to do. Make no mistake, José could spin a windy as well as the next one, but I grew to know him and could generally tell the difference. He also had a keen sense of historical values. He told me many times that I should put what he told me on paper "because when I am dead there will be none who remember these things."

One interesting fact that he told me was about the big arroyo that comes down through west Santa Barbara. Prior to El Gran Creciente, a big storm sometime in the 1870s, this was nothing but a cattle trail formed by the cattle coming down to the ciénega near the beach for water. During the year of the Gran Creciente there was a cloudburst in Salsipuedes Canyon and the rush of water cut the arroyo to near its present depth and size in a single night.

As to Joaquín Murieta, José scoffed at the idea that he was ever killed, as have some other old Californios that I have talked to. He said, "Muchacho, I knew him as well as I know you. He spent many nights at my father's home and I have sat and listened to his stories by the hour. He was a fine-looking man with fine features. I saw the head that they exhibited through the state and it was the typical flat-faced head of a cholo. The head exhibited with it was Three Fingered Jack who I also knew well, but the other was not Murieta's."

As to Fremont and the first American flag raised in Santa Barbara, he pointed out a spot in the middle of De la Guerra Street. There is a small adobe just east of the De la Guerra building. He measured out 18 paces from the southwest corner of this building and said, "This is where the first flag was raised. A man named Talo Pitín ran a cantina in the adobe where many were drinking that day. They attempted to run the flag up and the halyards stuck. Someone offered $10.00 to anyone who would climb the pole and free the halyards. A little Indian boy that I used to play with, who could climb like a monkey, went shinnying up the pole. Just as he got to the top the pole broke and he fell and was killed before my eyes, so it impressed it on my mind forever.

"The men freed the halyards, set the pole up again and raised the flag. It flew here for three days and then they moved it to the place where they now have a plaque."[1]

He then turned to me and said, "Muchacho, you should go tell the people who keep the historia del pueblo so that this can be a matter of record." I asked him if he had ever tried to straighten out a historian and he said no. I replied, "Neither did I and I am not going to start now. We both know it was raised so let's let it go at that."

As to grizzly bear, he told me many interesting stories which I will omit so as not to bore my readers. Two, however, are worth touching on very briefly. A short while before he died I took him for a ride in my car. We drove out between Santa Barbara and Montecito. There were at that time several acres of vacant land at the mouth of a gully where the gully spread out into a flat. There was a large clump of poison oak and yerba oso or bear brush growing in the flat.

"Here," he said, "is where I roped my first grizzly when I was about 14 years old. A group of us were riding together when some dogs we had with us started up a bear in that clump. We surrounded the clump and the bear charged out right at me. My father shouted 'Láselo,' meaning rope him. I was afraid of that bear but I was more afraid to disobey my father so I roped him. Others then got their reatas on him and we choked him to death."

At the time I visited José, he had been laid up for some months. His horse had fallen with him running down a hill on the island and he had been hurt so that he could not work. He was shipped over to Santa Barbara, where he finally got back into shape. He had then, instead of taking a bus or other modern conveyance, gotten hold of a horse and crossed the mountains and traveled all through the Cuyama, the San Marcos, and I guess a lot of other back country until he landed a job riding for some ranch. When I saw him he was cleaning up his equipment preparatory to going to work.

José told me that while he was in the back country he had seen two grizzly bears. I asked him if he was sure they were grizzlies and not black bears. He replied somewhat indignantly, "Do you think anyone who has caught as many grizzlies as I have would make that mistake?" I dropped the matter, thinking that perhaps the old man's memory was wandering into the long ago.

About ten years ago I read an article in the *Reader's Digest* which said that there was a strong possibility that grizzlies still existed in some of the remote spots back of Santa Barbara such as Sespe Canyon and in parts of Modoc County. Be that as it may, I hope that they were grizzlies that he saw and that the so-called sportsmen have not yet succeeded in killing the last of the species.

José was a grand old man and my friend. He could not read the printed page, but he could read a track in the dust as well as any Indian and taught me much about the art of tracking. He was an hombre del campo to the last. His stories lose much in being translated into everyday English. The old California poche, that mixture of early Spanish and Indian in which he told them, seemed to add flavor and romance to them.

Descanse en paz, amigo mío.

Note:

1. There are a number of stories surrounding Fremont's stay in Santa Barbara and the raising of the U.S. flag. There is a plaque commemorating the raising of the flag on the building at 819 State Street.

THE LAST TOMOLO

*T*omolos[1] were the large picturesque canoes made by the Indians of the Santa Barbara Channel and the offshore islands. The tomolos were the only canoes made by any of the California Indians. Some historians think that perhaps they got the idea from the Aleuts, who are known to have raided the California coast as far south as Mexico. Undoubtedly some of the Aleuts, intrigued by the climate, stayed here and added their blood and culture to the native stock.

The tomolos were described by Cabrillo when he sailed through the Santa Barbara Channel in 1542. They were large enough to carry twelve men, or more, pointed at both ends, and propelled by paddles. They were made of planks, which were of random lengths and widths. The Indians split the planks from driftwood, using any kind of wood that they could split and work with their stone wedges and obsidian knives. After laboriously fitting and shaping each piece, small holes were drilled along the edges and the plank literally was sewed in place by thongs. The finished tomolo is said to have had neither ribs nor framework. When finally sewed together, it was coated with tar, of which there were numerous deposits along the coast.

An interesting thing about the tomolos is that, in addition to being the only canoe made by California Indians, they were the only craft made in North America by this same unique method. Similar boats were found along the coast of Peru.

The result was a fast and seaworthy canoe. Cabrillo reports that the Indians had no trouble in keeping abreast of and even passing his sailing ships on their trip up the channel. The channel Indians were expert fishermen and relied on the ocean for a large part of their food. The tomolos made it possible for them to go far out to sea in search of fish.

It is known that they ventured as far out as San Nicolas and San Clemente Islands. They carried on a regular commerce with all of the Channel Islands, as well as up and down the coast. Most of the Indian mortars and pestles found along the channel coast are made of rock which the tomolos brought from Catalina Island. At least a large part of the white flint arrowheads found in California were made of flint brought from Santa Cruz Island. Many of them were made on the island.

I have visited many times what we called the Indian mines on Santa Cruz. These mines were large holes, big enough to bury an automobile, where the flint had been dug out of the surrounding volcanic rock. Lying about were innumerable broken and imperfect arrowheads as well as the chips flaked off in making the same.

The tomolos were used for a few years even after the Indians had been herded off to the missions and put to work at various occupations. Some may have been used to supply the missions and soldiers with fish.

Probably one of the last places that they were made and used was at Dos Pueblos, near Goleta. It was from here that what was probably the last tomolo in existence came, according to the story told me by at least three old vaqueros who worked under me on Santa Cruz Island.

In the 1830s, the Indians at some of the missions, including Santa Barbara revolted. It was a peaceful revolt in that the Indians, becoming tired of hard work, coarse food, and being locked in unventilated barracks at night all for the doubtful benefits promised them in the hereafter, just walked away.

This was followed by the hunting down and savage killing of Indians by drunken soldiers, a butchery that the padres were unable to prevent although they tried.[2]

Most of the Indians fled to the hills and some even crossed the mountains and never returned. Excepting for a handful, mostly old people, those living around Goleta were among the Indians who fled inland. The tomolos on the beach rotted away, were buried in the sands, or swept to sea by storms. Today a specimen of a tomolo reasonably intact would be worth a fortune.

In the 1860s and '70s, and probably earlier, vaqueros were already going out to the Channel Islands to round up cattle and shear sheep that had been allowed to multiply in a semi-wild condition. Among these were the old men from whom I heard this story.

When they and their companions landed at Prisoners' Harbor on Santa Cruz Island, probably in the late '60s or early '70s, an old Indian in a canoe that they described as being very large, made of different sized planks, patched with skins and tar and all sewed together with thongs, paddled down to Prisoners' Harbor from his camp a few miles east of that place. He greeted them with "Mielquieres" meaning in his broken Spanish, "I want honey," as he no doubt had greeted other Spaniards when they came to the island. He was already known as Mielquieres by the vaqueros, who had met him on earlier trips.[3]

As time went on and they saw Mielquieres on subsequent visits to the island, they gathered his story bit by bit. He had been taken from Santa Cruz Island together with his parents when he was a very small child. They were taken to the mission and became Mission Indians. He remembered very little about the island.

Before his parents died, they had told him many stories about their old home and always longed to return to it and the old life before the coming of the Spaniards. Mielquieres grew up with the same longing to leave the mission and to return to the island.

When the Indians revolted, or shortly thereafter, instead of going into the back country or attaching himself to some rancho, as so many Indians did, he went to the vicinity of Goleta. There he took one of the abandoned canoes and paddled over to Santa Cruz

Island, where he had lived ever since. His food consisted of fish, birds, seals, acorns, etc.

His description as given me was that of an old man of medium height, powerfully built, with long hair. His body and clothes reeked of fish and seal oil. He wore mostly cast-off clothing he had begged from the Spanish and had patched with skins. He lived in a small grass and tule hut at a spot a few miles east of Prisoners' Harbor, which is to this day called Mielquieres.

After hearing this tale, I rode over to where his camp had been with Cuate Espinoza. He showed me the approximate location and we both searched for some sign, such as a depression in the ground, foundation work, or mortars and pestles, but we found none. Probably others had carried off any relics that he might have left.

As to his ultimate fate, nobody knew anything. They saw him over a period of a few years on their infrequent visits to the island, when he came to the harbor saying "Mielquieres." After that they never saw him again. His tule and grass hut fell down and rotted away.

Probably Mielquieres and his tomolo were wrecked in one of the sudden squalls that come up on the Channel. I like to think that he and his tomolo, which was undoubtedly the last of its kind, were washed ashore and buried in the sands of his beloved island, to which he was the only one of his race to ever return.

I make no claim as to the historical correctness of the above story. An historian could probably punch it full of holes and any one who wants to is welcome so to do. It is based on the stories of old men who claimed to have known Mielquieres, the dates of the founding of the mission, the revolt of the Indians, and his probable age when my friends knew him. They all dovetail pretty well, including the location on the island that still goes by the name Mielquires. It is a legend that I like to believe.

Notes:

1. Although the original Chumash word is *tomol*, *tomolo* was a variant that for a time enjoyed popular and scientific usage.

2. McElrath is probably referring to the revolt of 1824, in which the Chumash at missions La Purísima, Santa Barbara, and Santa Inés took up arms. Order was not restored for over a month. At the end of the revolt, seven Chumash at La Purísima were sentenced to death and number of others received prison terms.

3. McElrath probably means, Melquiades, a fairly common Chumash neophyte name. The translation into "I want honey," does not seem to have factual basis. For the return of neophytes to the island see John Johnson, "An Ethnohistoric Study of the Island Chumash" (Master's thesis, University of California at Santa Barbara, 1982) on file at the Santa Barbara Museum of Natural History.

WILD BOARS

*S*anta Cruz Island has been famous for its wild boars for many years. They are not the European wild boar but descendants of domestic pigs that have gone wild and over a period of about one hundred years have reverted to the wild boar type with heavy shoulder plates, large tusks, small hindquarters, and evil dispositions.

The story is that domestic pigs were turned loose on the island in the 1860s. The idea was that they would grow and multiply on the acorns, manzanita berries, and other feed. It was probably a good idea with no coyotes, wolves, or mountain lions to bother them. Whether any of them were ever rounded up and taken to the mainland I never heard.

They did increase to the point where they became a nuisance and a major one. One or two large hogs in a single night would easily ruin a ton or more of grapes if they got into the vineyards. Multiply this by a dozen or more hogs and you get an idea of the damage they could do. When the grapes began to ripen we always kept one and sometimes two men patroling the vineyards at night with guns, to shoot any hogs they saw.

It was impossible to keep them out of the vineyards and fields. There was not a foot of barbed wire on the island. The Caires would not permit any barbed wire to be used and I think they were right. All of the fences around the vineyards, hay fields, and even a few small fenced pastures were made of smooth wire. Hogs, cattle, or sheep just walked up to these fences, poked their heads between the wires, and walked on through.

If you shot at a hog all the rest of the band took off on the run, generally downhill. When they came to a fence they didn't stop to poke their heads through. They just hit it running full speed. You could hear the wires snap like banjo strings and the next day there was a big job of fence repairing to be done.

The same thing was true of hay fields. We put our hay up in shocks to cure. A bunch of hogs would get into a hay field and start rooting under the shocks for grain. When they got through there would be hay trampled and scattered all over the place.

I remember coming in from the Christy Ranch late one bright moonlight night. Just before entering the Main Ranch yard the road ran between two rows of large eucalyptus trees. On one side was the creek bed and on the other a large hay field with the hay all cut and shocked. In the moonlight I could see about twenty hogs, most of them big ones, happily rooting up and scattering the hay. I could see them in the bright moonlight but as I was in the shadow of the trees they did not see me. I fired a couple of shots at them from my revolver. They still didn't know where I was so instead of going up the hill to the hole they had come in by they all started down the hill on the dead run straight for me. If I hadn't fired a couple of more shots and let out a whoop I think some of them might have run right over me. They hit the fence along the road and what a mess. It took two men a day to repair it.

We paid the men a bounty for every hog snout they brought in. I don't think the bounty had been changed or raised in fifty years. It was two Toscano cigars for each snout. Toscanos sold in the commissary two for a nickel. They were about seven inches long and crooked. The accepted way to smoke them was to break a cigar in two and smoke half of it at a time. I tried it a few times but never acquired a taste for them. The Italians wouldn't smoke anything else.

The methods of hunting wild hogs varied. Cuate Espinoza was good at bringing in fat pigs and sows for meat. They were not bad but as for the boars I would as soon try to eat a wolf. He had a small cur dog named Tiempo who was good at catching a small pig or sow by the ear and holding it until Cuate could catch it by the hind leg and kill it with his knife. Then Cuate dressed the pig, tied it behind his saddle, and brought it home for meat.

If it was a large pig, especially a boar, Tiempo bayed it but never closed in. He would bay it until Cuate got close and shot it. Tiempo had a lot of tusk scars and had learned not to tackle the big ones.

Pistola was another good pig dog. He acknowledged no one as his particular friend or master. He was very independent; but let anyone appear with a rifle and say "Vamos, Pistola" and he would hunt with that person all day. He was a very smart pig dog.

Pig dogs were a funny breed. The only good ones that I ever saw were small nondescript mongrels. Occasionally one of the men would get a bulldog or an airedale. They were all killed about the first big boar that they tackled. They were too brave and only had to get in reach of the boar's tusks once to be ripped wide open.

Tony Bonilla, the bull cook, was a crack shot with a rifle but rarely used one. He would take Pistola with him and whatever Pistola bayed regardless of size Tony would walk in and kill it with a home-made lance about six feet long. It was a dangerous sport because when one of those boars charged he came like a bullet and there was no stopping him. It was a case of side step in rough ground and do it fast.

Occasionally we would catch them in coyote traps. If the pig was of medium size we would put it in the pens at the ranch and fatten it on corn.

The big excitement was roping them. To do this one had to jump a hog in fairly clear level ground. A wild boar can give a saddle horse a good run for the first hundred yards or so. Down a steep hill he can run away from a horse. Uphill he is slow.

We never jumped a big hog in level open ground but what we went after him with our reatas . The instant you caught a hog you took your dallies on the saddle horn and started off on the run over rocks, cactus, and everything else. This was to knock the coraje (fight) out of him so he would not charge your horse.

There was another rule that was always followed. Whoever caught the hog, the man riding with him had to dismount, work up behind the hog, seize him by one hind leg and drive his knife into the hog's heart from behind the shoulder. A real playful trick was for the rider to give the hog two or three feet of rope about this time and then move up with his horse just fast enough to keep the hog a foot or two behind the man who was supposed to catch his hind leg and knife him. It really was funny to see what good time a bowlegged old cowpuncher could make with a big boar chasing him. Whether his chingaros and cabrones were louder than the laughs of any other riders who happened to be around is hard to say.

Roping a wild boar or pig is not the same as roping a steer or other domestic animal. It is necessary to catch them medio brazuelo, as the Spanish call it, which means by the neck and one front leg. Otherwise a hog will back right out of the loop even after it is tight. Purely by chance I made an exception to this on one occasion. I caught a large boar by the lower jaw. My loop tightened up behind his tusks and he was really caught. There was no pulling out of that one.

I had roped several boars on various occasions and then one day in Laguna when I was riding alone I had an experience that made me think twice before I would try it again. I was riding a fine big sorrel horse that was one of a number we had bought from the San Julian Ranch. I jumped a big boar on a piece of flat level grass land. The situation was ideal and I couldn't resist going after him with my reata.

I was closing in on him but was not yet close enough to throw my rope when he put on the brakes, turned and charged. My rope was useless so I dropped it and pulled my gun and started shooting at him. An island-raised horse would have dodged the boar with the speed of a cat. They had been raised dodging them. Alazan knew nothing about wild boars and made no attempt to dodge and I guess I was so busy shooting that I was slow in spurring him out of the way. As it was, the boar went right on under him between his front and hind legs and kept on going. As he passed he ripped a gash in one of the horse's hind legs about ten inches long and an inch deep. Fortunately he did not cut any arteries or tendons. Alazan made it back to the ranch, a distance of about ten miles, with very little loss of blood and hardly a lame step. I walked most of the way to make it easy for him. When we arrived at the ranch I washed out the cut and took some stitches in it. In a few days he was as good as ever.

As for the hog, he traveled several hundred feet before he dropped. When I examined him I found that I had hit him with five shots from a Colt .45, but none of them in a vital spot such as the head or the heart. Those boars, especially the big ones, are sure tenacious of life and hard to kill.

It made me think, however. It could have been the ruin or even the death of a fine horse if he had cut a tendon or an artery. I couldn't expect to be that lucky another time. I may have roped a couple more but I was less enthusiastic about it.

One day a group of us were moving cattle through the Portezuela when we jumped a large boar. He ran up into the thick manzanita brush on the south side of the valley with the dogs after him. We could tell from their barking that they had him cornered. I decided to go up after him and either get a shot at him or chase him down into the flat.

I started on foot up a narrow sheep trail through the manzanita and scrub oak. The brush was too thick and the trail too narrow to even attempt it on horseback. When I was about half way to the spot where I judged the hog to be he decided to come down the same trail that I was going up and he came like a bullet. I had no time to shoot and probably wouldn't have stopped him if I had hit him.

There was a small scrub oak leaning over the trail just where I happened to be. I grabbed a limb and jackknifed my legs up as high as I could just as the hog went under me. His shoulders hit me in the seat of my pants and almost knocked me loose from the tree.

The hog went down the trail and crossed the flat with a couple of men trying to get close enough to rope him. He made it ahead of them and into a small cul de sac, washout, or barranca. The barranca was only about ten or fifteen feet deep with perpendicular sides and he was trapped.

In the barranca was an accumulation of brush and leaning over the top of it a small willow. Ramón Romo climbed out on a willow limb to try to dangle a noose over the boar's head so he could be pulled out. About that time the willow limb broke off and as Ramón was lying at full length on the limb he was dropped head first into the barranca with the hog.

To get the full picture of this one had to know Ramón. He had a little of the grandee in him. He did everything with a flourish. If he was bucked off his horse the last thing he did as he went off was a flourish with his right arm and an "Ah, cabrón." From his tone it sounded like, "Just the way I planned it and I have the situation under complete control."

When he fell into the barranca there was the usual "Ah,

cabrón," as much as if to say "I've caught you now." For the next few seconds bedlam broke loose. The pig was squealing and grunting, the dogs yapping, and Ramón cursing. A couple of the men were standing on the banks above the barranca shouting advice to Ramón and hoping to get a shot at the boar without endangering Ramón. To be cooped up in a spot like that with a two-hundred-pound boar was no joke. I was sure that Ramón would be cut up by those sharp tusks.

About the time that I had crossed the flat to where the excitement was Ramón came out of the washout dragging the boar by the hind leg. Ramón didn't have a scratch on him. How he did it I don't know but as he dragged the pig into the open there was the usual "Ah, cabrón," which sounded like "See how easy it was."

I guided several parties of hunters who had received permission from the owners to hunt wild boars. One group wanted to hunt boars on motorcycles and came to the island with their motorcycles prepared to do so. One look at the country and they knew that would be impossible and were glad to go out on horses. Later one member of the party wrote a story for a magazine about wild boar hunting with motorcycles. It was a readable and interesting article but about ninety percent fiction.

I still have several wild boar tusks that I collected on the island. If any of my readers ever kill a large boar and want to save the tusks here is how you do it. Don't try to saw, chip, or pull them out of the jaw bone; you will only succeed in breaking them. Cut the lower jaw off of the boar and bury it in moist or wet earth for about two weeks. Dig it up and the tusks will practically fall out.

Wild boars are like any other wild animal. They will try to run away, but when cornered or wounded, they can be vicious fighters. Their speed in charging is surprising. I have seen dogs ripped wide open with one sidelong hook of their tusks. They can carry a lot of lead before they go down. My advice is the same to hunters of wild boars as to hunters of rattlesnakes. Get above them on the hillside if you are in anything resembling close quarters.

gorham ©

HERE AND THERE

There were many unrelated incidents and events that happened on the island. None of them were long enough or important enough to make a chapter but all I think worth recording. I am going to include them in a single chapter as they come to mind.

A short distance from Prisoners' Harbor on the way to Pelican Bay the trail passed close to the island cemetery. It was a small flat piece of ground neatly fenced and kept free of weeds and brush. There were about a half-dozen graves, each marked with a small wooden cross. All of these men had been buried many years before when the island was really isolated, with a boat calling once in two or three months.

The history of the graves I learned from Enrique Lopes, the blacksmith. About once a year Enrique would get hold of some extra wine and go on a two or three day bender. It usually happened on a weekend and on Sunday he always wound up at the cemetery, where he spent the day shedding tears and mourning over the graves of men he had never even known.

On Sunday morning on my way to Pelican Bay I ran into Enrique at the cemetery. "One poor fellow," he told me, "had gone to the Sur Ranch and had eaten thirty-six tomatoes and drank a gallon of wine. He died about an hour later." Who counted the tomatoes he didn't say.

Two others, according to his story, had gone to the Sur Ranch and gotten drunk. On the way home they were racing their horses in the dark and had hit the gate at the end of the callejón or lane. They were both thrown over their horses' heads and broke their necks. Two more were drowned and one died of natural causes. I continued my way to Pelican Bay for a swim and left Enríque weeping over the graves.

For minor cuts and bruises the men had their own remedies such as herbs, unto sin sal (unsalted beef kidney fat), etc., but occasionally I was called on to be doctor, nurse, and what have you.

There was the time that Ike Newton's horse fell on him and broke Ike's collarbone. It was winter and we had sent the *Santa Cruz* to San Pedro to have the bottom scraped and painted. She would be gone for at least two weeks. Ike's accident happened the day after she left.

I had an agreement with Ira Eaton, owner of the *Sea Wolf*, to call every three or four days with mail and to get a list of things we wanted from Santa Barbara. Ira was a happy-go-lucky sort and he did not show up for ten or twelve days.

In the meantime, I gave Ike first aid. I bandaged his shoulder with a pad in his armpit just as I had learned to do in first aid. I also had men out riding trying to hail a fishing boat or any sort of craft that we could use to take Ike to Santa Barbara. It was winter and there were no boats to be seen.

For ten days, Ike walked the floor at night. A broken collarbone is painful, as I know from experience. Ike lost about twenty pounds. He was afraid his collarbone might not heal properly and he would be crippled for life. Finally Eaton put in an appearance and I sent Ike to Santa Barbara. Dr. Bakewell X-rayed the break and said "There is nothing I can do for him—the break is practically healed and I couldn't have set it any better." Of course I didn't set it or make any attempt to do so. By good luck it set itself and my bandage held it in place. Ike returned, gained back his lost weight, and in a few days was back at work.

Hilario Lugo, an old vaquero, finally got too old to ride and I put him out at the Christy Ranch as cook. It was an easy job and he was happy to have it.

One day the foreman called me on the telephone and said that Hilario had run a sliver under his fingernail. He had dug at it with his knife and infected it and now had blood poisoning. The men had suggested various remedies which they had tried. The first was a bread and milk poultice. When this did no good somebody suggested a horse liniment poultice. This took all the hide off his hand and spread the blood poisoning. He now had swollen glands in his armpit and red lines running up the inside of his arm. The foreman wanted to know what they should do next.

I told him to put Hilario on a gentle horse and bring him to the ranch right away. I knew that once on a horse he would be able to make it faster and with greater comfort than in a wagon.

In the course of a few hours Hilario arrived at the ranch and the foreman with him. The last thing the men at the Christy did for him was to apply the last resort of some old-time cowboys. They put a poultice of fresh cow manure from his hand to his shoulder. He was a sweet-smelling mess. I cleaned him up and wrapped his arm in clean bandages soaked in boric acid. Then I put him on the boat for Santa Barbara. He was in bad shape and I thought, "Poor old fellow. The least that can happen will be that he will lose his arm."

I told the captain to get an ambulance or a taxi and send him to the hospital as soon as they arrived, also to get in touch with Dr. Bakewell and tell him to do everything possible for Hilario. I was really worried about him.

When the boat returned the next day my first questions were about Hilario and did they get him to the hospital, etc. The captain's son Pete answered me, "No, señor, when we pull up to the wharf that old man jump ashore and run like hell. When we get the boat tied up and I go after him I can't find him. Last night I hear that he is up at a bootleg joint and drunk like hell. I go up there after him but again I can't find that old Indian."

A couple of days later the boat had to make a trip to Santa Barbara so I told Pete to look for Hilario. "If he is still alive, send him to the hospital. If he is dead we will give him a decent funeral."

When the boat returned I asked about Hilario. Pete replied, "You don' need worry about that old Indian. He go to some old Indian woman and she put a poultice of yerbas on his arm and he is gonna be alright, but putah he is drunk." And so it was. In less than two weeks Hilario was back suffering more from a hangover than from his close brush with blood poisoning. Truly they were a tough breed.

There was a tragic epidemic that hit the island one year. It started at the Main Ranch. The first one to come down was a big strapping young Italian, a newcomer whose name I have forgotten. Several others came down in a few days. The symptoms were extreme lethargy and sleepiness. Thinking it might be biliousness, I gave them a laxative, which did no good.

The Italian boy got worse and worse until I realized he was in bad shape so I sent him to the county hospital. I visited him a few days later and they had him strapped in bed and he was raving, completely out of his head. He died a few days later.

When I arrived back at the island I received word that all three men at the Scorpion Ranch were very sick. I immediately got on my horse and headed for the Scorpion. I arrived a little before dark. All three men, Battlemini the foreman, Mennegazzo, his helper, and Dapelo, the cook, were all sick and slightly out of their heads. I saw that they had supper and then got them to go to bed. I then went to my cottage and turned in. It was an eerie place to be, miles from any help and with three men all slightly loco.

In the morning all three were much better and I felt that the emergency was past. I stayed around until after lunch and then started home. About an hour out of Scorpion I was seized with an overpowering drowsiness and headache. I finally had to get off my horse, tie him to a tree, and lie down on the ground, for as I thought, a half hour's sleep. When I woke up it was bright moonlight. I arrived home after midnight.

I felt better in the morning but was still pretty rocky. While I was eating breakfast the phone rang. It was Battlemini. He said he and Mennegazzo were much better, but that Dapelo was very sick. I ordered the schooner to go to Scorpion and pick Dapelo up and take him to the hospital. They did so and Dapelo died a couple of days later.

I wrote Dapelo's relatives on the mainland and the reply I received was short and direct, "How much money did he have?" The old fellow had about eleven thousand dollars in his savings account so I hope it made them happy.

My troubles were not over. When the boat reached Scorpion they had telephoned me that they had Dapelo on board but could not find either of the other men although they had searched the ranch, called, and blown the foghorn on the boat.

Dapelo they had found on the beach. He had evidently resisted the idea of going to the hospital so the others had carried him to the beach, hogtied him and left him for the schooner. Fortunately he had not been there too long when Pete Olivari landed from the boat and found him. Dapelo and Pete's family were old friends, so Dapelo went quietly aboard the boat with Pete. I told them to go on to Santa Barbara and I would come over to Scorpion and look for the men. I was still pretty shaky but I saddled up and set out for the Scorpion Ranch, fourteen miles away over the mountains. The trip wasn't bad as I was recovering fast. The sickness only lasted about three days in my case.

When I arrived at Scorpion I found both men up at the well pumping water. They were cutting wood and feeding it into the fire box of the old hot-air engine that we used to pump water with. There are probably not many people alive today who ever heard of one of those old engines, much less ever saw one in action. They probably hadn't been used or made for forty years even at that time. It was the only one I ever saw. As a very small boy I had seen advertisements and pictures of them in magazines.

Both men maintained that they had been there all morning and had seen nothing of the boat or the crew. They were very vague about Dapelo and how he happened to be hog-tied on the beach, but as they were both of them still half loco I took their word for what had happened and turned around and rode home. These men in their right minds were both kindly, decent sorts and would never have thought of hog-tying an old man and leaving him on the beach so I just wrote it off to la locura.

The doctors at the county hospital could not pinpoint the cause of the two men's deaths although they hinted it might be poison liquor or poison mussels. Dr. Kelly, the state health officer, came down from Sacramento with a couple of his aides. They visited the island and questioned me and several of the men. They had their minds made up before they came that it was poison liquor and that was the report they gave the Santa Barbara paper and I presume turned in to Sacramento in spite of the facts that I gave them, which were as follows.

The young Italian who died was an absolute teetotaler. He would not drink the thin, watered-down piquette that we served with lunch and dinner. It was against his principles. Dapelo was an old country Italian. He drank his bottle of piquette twice a day and that was all. As for me I had not had a drink of even piquette for a month or six weeks.

In those days doctors knew very little if anything about encephalo and called it meningitis or more often biliousness. Kelly was not equal to saying, "I don't know," so he said, "Poison liquor," and closed the case.

The epidemic passed and we had no recurrence of it other than that I could never convince any of my friends in Santa Barbara, including my brother-in-law, that we hadn't been running our own still and managed to turn out a batch of bad bootleg.

Cuate Espinoza was a great lover of dogs. He treated his dogs as though they were children—maybe better than a lot of parents treat their children. It was amusing to see him when his dog Tiempo did not mind him. He would grab a single wild oat straw and tell Tiempo he was a bad dog and he was going to give him a good whipping. He would then hit Tiempo two or three times with the oat straw. It was funny but it had it's effect. The dog would look contrite and mind the next time Cuate spoke to him. It was the same with horses. Every horse he rode soon became lazy. He was too kind-hearted to make them work.

But the other side of him was all Indian. A rustler was no more deserving of pity than a rattlesnake. A wild boar that injured his dog was something to be tracked down and killed if it took him all day and on one occasion all night.

One story that I heard and that he confirmed when I asked him about it concerned a large boar that killed his dog Nini. Cuate was riding to Christy Ranch one moonlight night. As he passed a fenced-in alfalfa field his dog Nini jumped a large boar in the field and took after it. The boar turned and killed Nini with one hook of his tusks.

Cuate was afraid that if he attempted to rope the boar at night he might get away. He circled the field all night keeping the boar in the alfalfa until daylight, when he roped him. He then tied him securely to a fence post and cut him to pieces bit by bit.

I have told this story not because I think it is entertaining but because it shows something of the mental workings of a breed of men raised in the open, without education or any refining influences and only a couple of generations at most removed from their wild Indian ancestors.

On the other hand Cuate supported a crippled brother in Santa Barbara on the meager pay of a vaquero and would give you the shirt off his back if he liked you.

One had to understand the old time Californios. Their virtues were the primitive ones of kindness, loyalty, generosity, and savagery.

After several months as bronco rider and cattle boss I had been promoted to superintendent. I still carried on with my original jobs plus the added duties of superintendent. I decided it was time to turn the bronco riding over to someone else. Things worked out perfectly. The corridas and shearing of the sheep and the roundup of the cattle were both finished and the vaqueros were returning to the mainland.

Tom Ward, a young vaquero and a good one, was anxious to stay on as a steady hand. His uncle, old Joe Espinoza, who was very fond of Tom, asked me if it would be possible to give Tom a steady job. I thought it over and told them that if Tom would tackle the job of riding a bunch of colts that were ready to break, I would give him a chance to see what he could do.

Old Joe spoke right up for him saying he would take the job on these conditions and that he, Joe, would instruct him and see that he made a good jinete (bronco rider). Tom just grinned and said, "I'll try it out, Mr. Mac." Tom was active, light, and wiry and I thought he had the nerve to make a good jinete. Events proved I was right.

We started right off the next morning. I picked a colt that I didn't think would buck too hard. We blindfolded it and put Tom's saddle and jáquima on it. Joe was there on his horse Favorita and he told Tom, "Don't be afraid. I will lead the colt off at a run and, if he gets to bucking too hard, I will pull him up in a circle and give you a chance to get set."

So Tom mounted the colt, set himself in the saddle, leaned forward, raised the blindfold, and gave the colt a jab with his spurs. The colt made a lunge and José, the ornery old Indian threw the lead rope away, let out a whoop, and gave the colt a crack with his quirt. Of course the colt started bucking and Tom instinctively grabbed the saddle horn. José who was riding right behind him, brought his quirt down across Tom's shoulders and cried "Suéltelo" (let go). Every time the colt showed an inclination to slow up José hit him a crack and every time Tom grabbed the saddle horn he hit Tom a crack.

Pretty soon the colt quit bucking. He wasn't too rough a bucker and Tom who was a good rider had managed to stay with him and by so doing gained a lot of confidence. Old Joe rode back now leading the colt and grinning from ear to ear. He had made un jinete of his nephew en la manera de los viejos (in the manner of the old timers) .

As for Tom, he came back with a grin on his face. I don't think he would have taken what he did from any one else than old Jose. He worshipped his uncle and, besides, he was as happy as a kid at having successfully ridden his first bronco with the prospect of a steady job. Tom went on to become a good bronco rider. I have seen him get on a real snaky colt on a cold frosty morning and ride him with a grin on his face.

Just to show how it is all in what one is used to: Tom went to Santa Barbara for a few days. When he came back he asked me what sounded like an innocent question, "Did you ever play football, Mr. Mac?" When I told him that I had played a lot of football he shook his head and said, "I saw my first football game while I was in Santa Barbara. I wouldn't play that game for ten thousand dollars. It's too rough."

The next morning he was riding a bucking, pitching bronco and enjoying it.

Over the years the custom had grown up on the island that when the corridas were finished and the vaqueros were paid off to return to Santa Barbara each man was allowed to buy at wholesale price up to ten gallons of wine to take home with him. This was delivered to the schooner along with all of their belongings or muchillos.

Of course they drank a lot of the wine between the island and Santa Barbara. When they arrived at Santa Barbara all who were able to climb onto Stearns wharf with their jugs did so. One or two generally couldn't make it until the next day. Those that did make it were met by their compañeros and all had to have a traquito (a little drink) or two to celebrate the home coming. I imagine a lot of the wine never got as far as State Street in the original container.

Sooner or later tragedy was bound to strike. On one of the trips a vaquero who shall be nameless fell overboard. He was a strong swimmer like all of the Spanish who were raised on the Santa Barbara waterfront. If they had left him alone it is highly possible he would have swum the rest of the way. The boat put about and picked him up.

Someone in the group insisted that the only way to treat a drowning man was to roll him over a barrel. So, in spite of his protests, they grabbed his arms and legs and started sawing him back and forth over a barrel. This they continued until they arrived in Santa Barbara. When they tied up at the wharf the poor devil was dead. Another case of the patient's being killed by well-meant but ignorant first aid.

This happened the year before I went to the island. What the captain and crew were thinking about I don't know. They were probably afraid of that wild bunch. This tragedy plus prohibition put an end to the old custom of selling them wine. It also probably made lower State Street a more quiet spot when the vaqueros returned from the island.

Isolated and far behind the times as the island was, it was also a demonstration of how a group living as we did could learn to make do with what we had. Felix Mauri, who was foreman at the Scorpion when I first came to the island, would gather olives by the sackful at Smugglers' Cove every year. From these he would make gallons of very good olive oil, enough to supply the entire island for a year. He also preserved a quantity by the old Spanish water method. Incidentally they were the best olives I have ever eaten.

Casi, an Italian, was born a cheesemaker. He worked at the

Christy Ranch. Casi gentled and trained several range cows. He would get up a couple of hours early in the morning and milk his cows before breakfast. Then he would put in a day's work in the fields. After supper he would again milk his cows and then repair to an old adobe where he had built himself a crude brick stove and by the light of a kerosene lantern busy himself making cheese until ten or eleven o'clock. He kept the entire island supplied with a very good quality of California jack cheese.

I also got into the act of make-do. When I came to the island they had a couple of small wheel tractors that were used for plowing, etc., in the hay fields. One day while we were moving a tractor from the Main Ranch to the Christy, it got away from the driver and plunged down a steep hillside about one hundred feet into a ravine. It turned a couple of somersaults on the way but came to rest upright in the bottom of the canyon. The driver, Mennegazzo, jumped clear and was uninjured, but the tractor was beyond repair as a tractor. Fortunately the engine was unharmed.

The wharf at Prisoners' Harbor had been in need of new piling for several years. We had an old pile driver that was operated by a team of horses. The hammer would be drawn to the top of the tower and then it was automatically released by a pair of sister hooks and bam! It came down on the pile from a height of twenty feet and really drove the pile. There was, however, no way of regulating the blow. It was necessary to leave the piles sticking up in the air from five to six feet above the pier. It was then necessary to sling a platform over the edge or under the pier so that men with crosscut saws could cut the piles to the desired length. This was slow and tedious. Perhaps that was why repairing the wharf had been put off on one excuse or another.

I took the engine out of the wrecked tractor, bought a winch and some cable, remodeled the old pile driver, and built a new one. With this we could either wallop the piles to drive them down or tap them gently to the exact height that we wanted. It saved a lot of time and labor.

It also brought forth from B. Crofton Atkins, a very likeable Englishman who was my assistant at the time, some pertinent remarks. He asked me if I had ever worked on a pile driver. I told him that I had never had any experience along that line and he replied in his precise English accent, "Ah, you Americans! You astound me. In England if we want shoes put on a horse we send for a farrier of years' experience. You shoe your own horses. If we want piles driven we send for a man who has served a proper apprenticeship and then had years of experience. But you, without a day's experience, you build a pile driver and the damn thing works so you rebuild a wharf."

In the early Spanish days Santa Cruz Island was made a Spanish penal colony. That is how Prisoners' Harbor got its name.[1] Criminals were put ashore, given a few tools, provisions, and cattle and left to work out their own salvation. This they did by slaughtering the cattle and making skin boats with which they escaped to the mainland, according to the stories and legends.

I have never heard of any tools, equipment, or artifacts being found on the island that could be traced back to the inhabitants of the penal colony, with one possible exception. This exception is based on a story told me by Cuate Espinoza.

For many years he told me he had seen the remains of an old carreta or two-wheeled cart on a hillside between Prisoners' Harbor and Pelican Bay. It had solid wooden wheels and was fastened together with wooden pegs. The axles were also wooden. If it had ever been reinforced with rawhide that had long since disappeared when he first saw it. Cuate felt sure it was a remnant of the penal colony. He had suggested several times that it be taken to the ranch and preserved as it was gradually rotting away where it was. No one seemed interested and nothing was ever done about it. A year before I went to the island a brush, grass, and forest fire swept the island from Prisoners' Harbor to Pelican Bay. In this fire the last vestiges of the carreta were burned.

Fighting amongst individuals is something that is generally expected in a group of men living together on a ranch or in a construction camp. I have seen a fair amount of it on other ranches and in construction camps. I have even been mixed up in one or two myself.

On the island I never saw blows struck but twice. One of these fights was pure comedy. The other could have been tragic if allowed to continue. A third never got to the fighting stage but it too had an element of childish comedy.

Abelino Lugo, the stableman and general chore man, was a dour old Santa Barbara Spaniard. When a young man a horse fell on him and broke Abelino's leg. He had lain in an arroyo for three days before they found him. The leg was probably badly set if at all and as a consequence was crooked and he walked with a limp. Add to this a pair of loose bib overalls tied around the middle with a strap for a belt, a large sombrero, and handlebar mostachos and you have the picture.

One of his daily chores was to hitch his old horse Lucifero to the timbarol or dump cart and haul the garbage from the kitchen. Abelino kept Lucifero fat and shiny and, although the horse was old enough to vote and had at some time been foundered, leaving him stiff as a poker, he always arched his neck and tried to prance with the timbarol rattling behind him. It was the same when Abelino saddled him in the morning to bring in the milk cows. He pranced and tried to act like a young cow pony. According to some of the older men on the island he had at one time been one of the best on the island.

How the feud between Abelino and the cook started I don't know. When Abelino came up to the kitchen in the morning Pico would stand in the doorway of the kitchen and Abelino beside his timbarol and they would tell each other off. I sometimes had to go out and tell them to shut up and get back to work.

One morning when I stepped out of the office to tell them to cut it out I saw Pico as usual in the kitchen door and Abelino beside his dump cart. The only difference was that Abelino had a large single action .45 hanging from his belt. I walked over to Abelino and asked what was the idea of his having his gun with him. He replied, "Pico say he gonna keel me some day."

I answered, "Pico is not going to kill anybody. Go down to the barn and put that gun away."

Abelino pondered a few seconds and then said, "You sure Pico not gonna keel me?"

"Yes," I told him, "I am sure Pico is not going to kill you."

"Awright, I take my gun off," and down to the barn he went and put his gun away. The funny part was that that ended their battles of words.

At Prisoners' Harbor we had an Italian named Novero who

acted as caretaker. One of his jobs was to catch the lines thrown from the schooner and make them fast, etc. The job did not entail much work and was a sort of a pension.

One morning Novero called me on the telephone and in a state of great agitation told me that Mike Nigro, a young, aggressive Neapolitan, who at the time was captain of the *Santa Cruz*, had gotten mad and beat him up. I went down to the harbor and found Novero in his house still pretty well shaken up but showing no signs of having been beaten up. Of course Novero started in on his version of the vicious, unprovoked and brutal assault Nigro had made on him. I told him to come with me and we would talk to Captain Mike, assuring him that I would let them both tell their sides of the story.

The boat was tied to the wharf, as it was her day to go to Santa Barbara. They were waiting for me to arrive with the mail, etc. Captain Nigro was waiting on the wharf. As we approached he said, "It didn't amount to anything, Mr. Mac. He called me some names and I slapped his face."

Novero, who could not speak a word of English, thought Captain Nigro might be building too strong a case for himself so he stepped between us saying in Spanish, "Dispénseme, dispénseme" (excuse me, excuse me) .

"O.K." Mike said, "Let him tell his side of it" and stepped back with his hands on his hips.

Novero assumed a squatting position on the wharf and started his explanation speaking in Spanish. He pointed to a spot on the wharf and said, "He was here"; then turning in a quarter circle so that his left side was toward the captain he said, pointing to another spot, "And I was here," and POW! He came up from a squatting position with a full right-hand swing literally from his heels and caught Captain Nigro flush on the chin. Down went the captain more surprised than hurt. If he had been two feet closer to the edge he would have gone into the water.

Nigro came to his feet and if you ever saw a mad dago he was it. If I hadn't grabbed and held him there is no telling what he would have done. He was kissing the tips of his fingers and blowing the kiss to heaven accompanied by a steady string of "Cristo la Madonnas, Dagoin so and sos" as well as some choice

English expletives.

As for Novero as soon as he hit the captain he had taken off for his house on the run. One thing that added to the comedy was that a few days before Novero had dropped a heavy weight on his foot and succeeded in smashing a toenail. He had wrapped his foot in a couple of yards of bandage and on top of that a gunny sack to keep it clean. It made his foot look about four times its natural size. As he ran he stopped every little way to look back and in so doing gave one of the best amateur imitations of Charlie Chaplin that I ever saw.

I was still holding Captain Nigro but couldn't help laughing uproariously. I guess my laughter must have been contagious because pretty soon the captain began to laugh too.

I sent him off to Santa Barbara and told him to buy a drink when he got there for himself and the crew on me. I knew that by the next day he would have cooled down.

When I went back to Novero's house, a one-room affair with one door, he had about all the furniture he possessed piled against the door and through a window I could see him sitting in a chair at the back of the room with a double-barreled shotgun across his knees. It took a lot of talking to get him to unbar the door and put his shotgun away, even after I assured him that Captain Nigro and the schooner were well on their way to Santa Barbara.

The following day when Novero sighted the schooner about an hour and a half out of Prisoners' Harbor he got in his old Petaluma cart and came to the Main Ranch literally on the run. As he whirled into the ranch yard he shouted, "Viene el barco, viene el barco" (the boat is coming, the boat is coming) for all the world like Paul Revere announcing the coming of the British. I spent another half hour getting him to come down to the harbor with me. The captain landed with a grin and shook hands with Novero. That ended that.

Sometime after I had left the employ of the island company I returned with Mr. L. W. Symmes to help him make a report on the island, which he had been appointed to do by the Superior Court in San Francisco. An elderly man named Revel had taken my place as superintendent.

While Mr. Symmes and I were there some of the men had broken into Mr. Caire's private wine cellar and stolen a quantity of wine. About half or more of the men were really high for several days.

Ramón Romo had gotten more than his share and developed a fight drunk. One evening at the supper table he kept needling and insulting a big husky young Italian to the point that when they came out of the dining room the Italian grabbed Ramón and shook him and slapped his face. Ramón broke loose and announced that he was going to the bunkhouse for his gun. A minute later he emerged with a Colt .45 in his hand.

By that time everyone including the superintendent had taken refuge inside or behind the adobe buildings. Ramón started on the hunt for the Italian who had slapped him. I knew that old Yaqui and knew that if he found him he would probably shoot him and maybe a couple of innocent people to boot.

Everybody had disappeared from view and even though I had nothing to do with running things I felt it was up to me to corral the old Indian. I also felt that as we were old friends and had ridden many days together that the last thing Ramón would do would be to shoot me. I was right. When I walked up to Ramón and said, "Give me your gun, Ramón," he surrendered it with no more protest than to drunkenly declare that I was the only person in the world that could take his gun without getting shot, etc., etc. I think that like so many people who go on a rampage looking for trouble he was secretly hoping someone would stop him. I led him into the bunkhouse where he flopped on his bed and passed out for the night.

No, Ramón did not get fired. He was assigned to manual labor in the vineyard, which was a big come down for a rider. Of course he quit before long of his own accord. I gave him back his gun a few days later with a friendly lecture before I left the island. I have never been back since.

Undoubtedly things have changed. The old Spanish riders and their California poche, the old Spanish language of California, have all long since ridden to the last roundup. The old Italian vineyard workers who spent their lives on the island and spoke no English are gone too. Methods have changed and been modernized.

A few of the young men, old men now, may still be around Santa Barbara and remember the old days. They were good days.

Note:

1. In 1830, a Mexican prison ship released a number of convicts on Santa Cruz Island, after being denied permission to do so at San Diego and Santa Barbara. Reportedly, most of the prisoners eventually made their way back to the mainland. The spot where the prisoners were released came to be known as Prisoners' Harbor.

THE AUTHOR

$\mathscr{I}$ was born the youngest of eleven children, seven of whom are still living, on a ranch of several hundred acres on the outskirts of North Temescal, California. Temescal was a small town between Oakland and Berkeley. We had orchards of cherries and apricots as well as numerous individual trees such as apples and plums. There were also hay fields and truck gardens. The truck gardens were farmed by Chinese. We had dogs, family cows, chickens, and saddle horses. I learned to ride at a very early age. My Dad said that I rode like a Comanche. This was due to his wisdom in making me ride bareback with nothing but a rope looped around the horse's nose. Like the rest of my brothers and sisters I got thrown or "piled," as we called it, more than once while learning. I learned to use an ax, climb trees, and do all of the chores that went with country life as well as having a lot of fun playing with my brothers and sisters.

I also learned to rope when I was just a small boy by practicing on the horses, dogs, and cows, and even got so I could rope chickens. I also practiced on Ah Joe, a friendly good-natured Chinaman. Ah Joe would run away from me and then laugh and think it a great joke if I caught him. It was a wonderful life for a small boy.

In my early teens I started working during vacations and sometimes on Saturdays and after school. My jobs were varied. I worked as a laborer on the Sheldon Building in San Francisco when it was built in 1907. I clerked in a store, as a baggage smasher for Wells Fargo, as an office boy, and during the school term riding an occasional bronco for anyone who wanted a horse broken. There was one summer when I rode as a ranger for the Peoples Water Company on the hills back of Oakland and Berkeley. Where I rode is now all subdivided and covered with homes.

Weekends I drove cattle for Newman and Korn, who had a slaughterhouse back of Mills College. We would drive them from as far as Mount Diablo and Walnut Creek or from Newark or

Milpitas in bunches of from half a dozen to twenty-five or thirty along such roads as the Foothill Boulevard or over the Summit Road back of the Claremont Hotel. Today these roads are heavily traveled and in some cases four lane highways. We didn't see an automobile once in half an hour—so seldom in fact that our horses were scared to death of them.

I managed to squeeze in time to play football all through my high school, playing both American and rugby. I also put in a lot of time at wrestling and gymnastics. This has saved me many hard falls in my riding since then.

And so I drifted through my first three years of high school with little ambition other than to get good enough grades to allow me to play football, varying the monotony by making my teachers' lives miserable, at which I was an outstanding success. I saw no chance of going to college. My family could not afford to send me and I didn't see how I could finance myself. It was before the day of easy scholarships for everything from athletics to tatting. My future was finish high school and find a job.

Some angel in disguise—he or she must have been an angel because my coterie of friends at that time did not include any angels recognizable as such—advised me to see George Dickie, the Superintendent of the Recreation Department of the City of Oakland. I did so and he hired me on the spot to work Saturdays and Sundays. George was and is a wonderful person and a warm friendship started that still endures. He was not easy on me. My first assignment was to take charge of the toughest park in Oakland. It was a Sunday ball park where semi-professional teams played. My job was to put a stop to fighting, gambling, and drinking, a fair-sized assignment for a nineteen year old. I was a big husky kid with a good pair of fists which I knew how to use. I beat a couple of the rowdies at their own game and from then on I had no trouble.

The big thing was the change it made in my own outlook on life. I now saw a chance to go on to college so overnight I became a model student, taking extra courses and getting good grades. I think some of my teachers grew to like or at least tolerate me. My work with the Recreation Department put me through the last year of high school and three years of college, allowing me to save enough to finance my last year.

Before entering college I took six months off from the Recreation Department and went to work on a surveying gang. We were surveying the line for the Big Creek and Dawn Railroad in what at that time was a wilderness in the High Sierra. We spent the winter at from 4,000 to 8,000 feet elevation, living in tents. It was an interesting experience and I learned a lot.

In college I did not go out for athletics. I didn't have the time and my work for the Recreation Department made me a professional. I did enter one boxing tournament which I won but was disqualified from any additional tournaments because of my professional status. They were stricter in those days.

In my senior year I stayed out for six months and worked for the Whitehall Estates at Tracy. This was a large corporation ranch and I did everything from common labor to driving four- and six-horse teams hauling hay and grain. I wound up timekeeping and doctoring sick cattle and horses as a side line. It was good experience.

After college my friend George Dickie and I bought an eighty-acre farm on the Yuba River. A farm is hardly the right name for it. It was eighty acres covered with willows and some cottonwoods as thick as the hair on a dog's back, no house, no well, and the nearest neighbor a mile away, but lots of rabbits, quail, and rattlesnakes.

I hired a wagon and moved in with a group of about six laborers that I picked up in Marysville. The first few nights we slept on the ground until we got our tents, including a cook tent, set up. I sunk a drive point well outside the cook house door and this with a hand pump was our water supply.

To make a long story short we grubbed the trees and brush out by hand, piled and burned them, leveled the land, installed a gasoline engine and pump on the river, and planted beans. During the fall I built a fourteen by fourteen cabin. To use the words of one hired hand to describe it, "She ain't much for looks but she's hell for stout." I spent the winter in my cabin alone. I also built a barn for my hay and my horses.

It was all a wonderful experience in pioneering but World War I was on. I being a farmer was exempt from the draft. However I was single and it looked like too good a brawl to miss so with my partner's blessing we leased the ranch and I told the draft board to send me to camp. They did so the next day.

I was sent to Camp Kearny, where I became a machine gun sergeant and also won the light heavyweight championship of the camp on a decision. I later lost it back to the man I won it from by a close decision. I never got to go overseas. I have always regretted this as it was what I had enlisted for. But such is fate.

After my discharge I took the first job that came along. I went to work in the shipyards as a boilermaker's helper. After a one week apprenticeship I went to another shipyard and hired on as an experienced boilermaker. I got away with it for a month, until I landed the job on Santa Cruz Island.

I must confess at this point that it was not wholly due to my own knowledge of boilermaking that I lasted. It was probably due to the luck of the Irish. My first night when I reported to the foreman on the graveyard shift, who should be standing talking to him but an old friend of mine, Red Baldwin, an ex-big-league ball player. We greeted each other warmly and the foreman asked me if I wanted Red for my helper which of course I did.

As soon as the foreman was out of earshot Red told me "From here out you are an ex-ball player. The foreman is a baseball nut and as soon as all the machines are going we go up to his shack where there is a stove and we entertain him with baseball stories for most of the shift." Of course I did not pose as a big leaguer; he might have looked up the records. I just followed Red's lead and laughed and remembered the incidents he told about. I hope I may be forgiven the tall tales I acquiesced in, but it meant many an hour beside a stove in a warm shack instead of out in the cold running a punch.

I left the island to take a position as assistant manager of a very large cattle ranch in Chihuahua, Mexico. The promises were glittering, but when I arrived in Mexico—which was torn by revolution and where no law existed except that which you carried on your hip—my wife and I (we were married just before leaving for Mexico) soon found out that they meant nothing. I had just been sent there as a club over the incumbent manager's head. So in a short while it was back to the United States.

Once back in the U.S., with a wife to support, a job was the important thing. Some of my jobs were working for a paving company, riding in the movies, a job with a mining company, and finally winding up as manager of a large raisin and fig ranch in the San Joaquin Valley.

After that I became an appraiser for the Federal Land Bank for a number of years. I took a leave of absence from the Land Bank to become superintendent of the Jacks and Thomas interests in Monterey County, which consisted of large ranch properties. I held this position for thirty years until after the death of the last member of the families, when most of the lands went to the University of California, Stanford and Caltech.

For twenty years I have been raising cattle. That is now my occupation with some writing and appraising as a side line.